Growing (UP) at Thirty-Seven

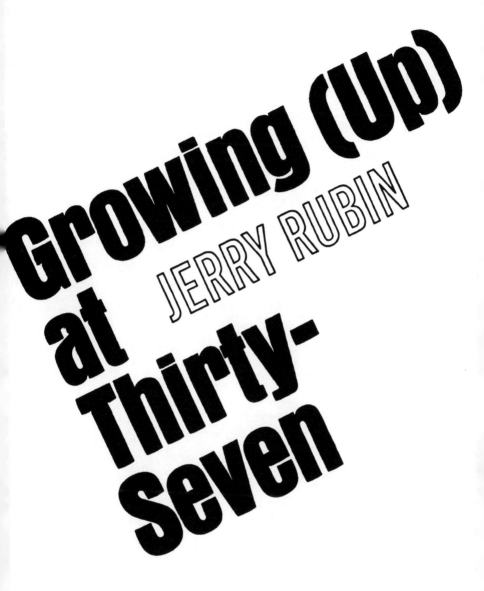

Growing (Up) at Thirty-Seven

JERRY RUBIN

M. EVANS
Lanham • New York • Boulder • Toronto • Plymouth, UK

M Evans
An imprint of Rowman & Littlefield
4501 Forbes Boulevard, Suite 200
Lanham, Maryland 20706
www.rowman.com

10 Thornbury Road, Plymouth PL6 7PP
United Kingdom

Distributed by National Book Network

LIBRARY OF CONGRESS CATALOGING IN PUBLICATION DATA
Rubin, Jerry.
  Growing (up) at thirty-seven.
  1. Rubin, Jerry. 2. Radicalism—United States.
I. Title.
HN90.R3R88   322.4'2'0924   75-31572
ISBN 978-1-59077-291-1

Design by Joel Schick

Manufactured in the United States of America

Contents

Acknowledgments

This book could in some ways be called a
cooperative venture because of the valuable
feedback I received from friends in many months
at the typewriter. I want to acknowledge the
editorial assistance of Russ Schoch, David Weir,
Anne Valley Fox, Diane Rose, Diane Sward, Craig
Pyes, Claude Steiner, Neil Anderson, Michael
Kennedy, Eleanor Kennedy, Michael Lerner, Lanny
Cotler, Steve Cotler, Fred Cody, Sam Keen, Nancy
Kurshan, Jerelle Kraus, Phyllis Greene, Jerry Mander, Ken
Kelley, Suzanne Wexler, Stella Resnick, Jerry
Kamstra, Abe Peck, Sara Straus, Miriam Glaser,
Diane Romanchuk, John Brockman, Arlene
Bechek, Marv Treiger, Ronnie Davis, Sharon Skolnick,
Steveann Fink, Dana Middleton, Helen Tworkov, John
Katz, Stew Albert, Stan Jackson, and Richard Levine.
I have changed the real names of some of the people in
this book because I feel that I have no right to invade
their privacy with my revelation of intimate details of
their lives; what is important is what happened, not their
specific identity. This book is a subjective history of my
experience in the external and internal movements. In
no way can I acknowledge all the people who contributed
to my growth and to the political movement.

With love to my mother and father and brother Gil

Chapter 1

Crying at My Own Funeral

I N 1970, at the age of thirty-two, I had everything I thought I wanted in life. I was a leader in a powerful political movement struggling to transform our country's institutions. I loved and enjoyed the love of a warm woman. I had written a best-selling book and was a folk hero of rebellion to young people. My life was exciting, involved, relevant. I had satisfied all my childhood dreams. And then: crash.

In two brief years the mass political movement disappeared and the woman left me. A group of young kids publicly retired me from the movement for being over thirty. My fame turned to notoriety and "Where is he now?" stories. Newspapers began describing me with adjectives like "erstwhile" and "aging." People began relating to me as an image, not as a human being. Worst of all, I myself believed the image; I forgot who I was. I felt dead at thirty-four.

But I didn't take it all personally. What happened to me happened to thousands of people who believed we were making a political and cultural revolution in the 1960's. Suddenly the movement was over, and where were we?

One day, as I was walking down the street in New York, an insight zapped me. I was being given an opportunity to grow. If I didn't stay stuck in old images, I could start my life all over, expand into new areas, reincarnate myself. So, I started examining myself in every aspect of my life.

First: personal relationships. Ruthie and I were movement sweethearts. We met a few weeks before the first big Berkeley antiwar march in October, 1965, and hung out together at every demonstration, meeting, press conference, and riot for the next five years. Ruthie and I were totally loyal to each other; she was my partner for life.

One afternoon in September, 1970, Ruthie burst into the room, looked into my face, and said, "When you were in jail, I was with Arnie. I love him and want to go live with him."

If words can bring instant psychic cancer to one's nervous system, "Good-bye, I'm leaving," will do it. A shock of pain paralyzed my entire body. The next day I furiously destroyed my apartment, running through it naked, crying, screaming, at the top of my lungs. I alternated between rage and getting down on my hands and knees to beg Ruthie to stay. I was mad, insane; I could not bear to be alone and insisted that friends sleep over to keep me company. People I knew feared I might commit suicide.

Ruthie disappeared with her suitcases and never came back. Five years of intense daily companionship ended in an instant. I was alone, and badly shaken.

With Ruthie gone, I could not eat or sleep or talk. I fantasized about her night and day. Every woman in the street looked like her. I was shit because she left me. Life had no meaning, only pain and suffering. There would never be another for me like Ruthie. I kept saying to myself, "If only I had done things differently."

In retrospect I realized that our relationship, however special it seemed to me, reflected the male domination of the society around us. Since what I was doing was so "politically important," Ruthie took the role of Mama, supporting me when I was down, feeding me, buying my clothes, washing my underwear, typing my manuscripts.

It is frightening to discover that another person is essential to your survival. Was what I called love really fear? For five years we had presented ourselves to our friends as a "couple"; now I had to begin thinking of myself again as a single individual.

At times, though, even in the midst of my suffering, I understood that I had used our relationship as a hiding place, avoiding women behind the protection of one woman. I resolved to look honestly at my relationships with women, to find out why I needed a woman to survive. Simultaneously, however, I began looking

3

for another Ruthie. Could I ever trust a woman again? Could I ever love again?

At the same time my personal life was falling apart; it was getting tough to be a hero. People expected me to be superhuman. I had become a symbol for thousands of young people, which made me feel good, but also increasingly uneasy. I received about a dozen letters a day from kids who told me they wanted to run away from home to join the revolution: "Please answer this letter. I will never believe in the revolution if you don't. I need to know that you exist."

After the movement died down, I became paranoid. "Does that person love me, or my name?" I didn't know who to trust. I was scared to sleep with a woman because I feared she'd spread it around if I were a lousy lay. Part of me still loved to be recognized by strangers, but I found myself with many acquaintances and few friends. Once I had loved being a living martyr; now I hated being a big name from the past.

No one seemed to see my pain, my anxieties, my terror—all they saw was an "image." Some saw me as an aging baseball hero who had lost his fast ball or a rock star with one big hit who had faded. Some saw me as the romantic embodiment of their beautiful lost youth. Some saw me as Frankenstein.

Many people regarded me as their moral spirit— strangers spent hours apologizing to me for not having been active in the movement. The existence of my myth had liberated thousands of people to be themselves, but I had to live my own life.

I found out something else about being a hero: followers of heroes have a hidden desire to see their heroes die. Young kids came to praise and then looked for things to prove that I was phony. The only heroes that survive are dead. Young kids wanted me dead, or at least in jail.

In the 1960's I helped create a cultural model and a national youth organization, the yippies. I participated in the early stages of the antiwar movement, from troop-train demonstrations and mass marches to civil disobedience, in Berkeley from 1965 to 1967. I helped organize the October, 1967, march on the Pentagon, and was one of the organizers of the Chicago demonstrations during the 1968 Democratic Convention. I was on trial with seven others for five and a half months in the conspiracy trial that became a national symbol of resistance. For eight years, I was busy day and night in political activity, and I helped develop a style of guerrilla theater, humor, and politics.

For years I had successfully manipulated the media to serve the antiwar movement. Now I found myself a victim of the media: people saw me as crazy, dangerous, violent, insane. The image was driving me mad, until I realized that I believed it, too. As long as I believed I was a revolutionary hero, I would criticize myself for not fulfilling my own self-image. I had to free myself from me.

One Sunday in October, 1972, on the way to a five-hour massage class in the afternoon and, later, supper with Ram Dass, I left my house in New York's SoHo district and walked to my car. Suddenly, I stopped short, my eyes burning at the sight in front of me. My car had been mugged; it stood in a pool of shattered glass. My body stiffened with rage. Who had done this? A crackpot? a hard-hat? a right-winger? Was someone trying to get *me*?

5

Jerry Rubin

Later, through the underground grapevine, I learned that the assault on my car was done by younger yippies who called themselves "zippies" ("Put the zip back into yip!") to declare their independence from me, Abbie Hoffman, and the other older yippies.

I let my legs take me to massage class. An hour later, instead of trembling in the war zone of a New York street, I was nude with thirty other people and we were preparing our sheets and massage oils. As the guinea pig for the day, I relaxed into mental nothingness while three people massaged my legs and back. Every so often I flashed on my demolished car, but it's hard feeling angry when someone is stroking your ass!

A few hours later I went to see Ram Dass and told him what happened. "If you find them again at your car," he said, "and want to beat them up, do it with love." And then he told me a Zen story I have never forgotten. A man searched the world to find the killer of his wife. Finally he found him and chased him down an alley. He pulled out a knife to kill him, when suddenly the killer spat into his face. The man put the knife away, turned around, and walked away. Asked later why he did not kill his wife's murderer, he said, "Because I got angry."

Ram Dass and I began looking into each other's left eye without saying a word. As I looked into his eye, I first saw Ram Dass, then a universal eye, then the entire world, then the person who had demolished my car. I knew that I had driven that person to smash my car, and that beyond our personalities we were the same. Ram Dass, for a moment, was the person who smashed my car. For a fleeting instant, I wished I could find the car-rapist and look into his eyes and connect with his fear, his anger, and his love.

The attack on my car had a political motivation. I had been unwilling to drop out as leader of the yippies. I went to Miami Beach for the 1972 Republican and Democratic Conventions, hoping that history would create another Chicago and I would again be in the center of the action.

In Miami a faction of the yippies called me a sellout because I stayed in a hotel rather than in a park. On my thirty-fourth birthday, July 14, 1972, these zippies marched to my hotel armed with a cake to throw in my face to celebrate my retirement from the movement, because I was over thirty! Quite a karmic irony for someone who had helped popularize the slogan "Don't Trust Anyone Over 30." The zippies used the same media tactics on me that I and others had used against LBJ and Nixon.

"YIPPIES ATTACK YIPPIE LEADERS RUBIN AND HOFFMAN FOR BEING OVER 30." The media ate it up.

Young kids who had seen my painted face on the cover of *Do It!* expected me to spend the rest of my life running naked through the streets. The fact is, I was always more sane and middle class than my yippie image.

I had become a father figure to thousands of young people. They wanted me to show them direction, and at the same time, they hated me, much the way a son hates his father. They would both ask for my autograph and spit in my face, exaggerating my importance and attacking me for letting them down.

Everybody except the government officials, with whom my myth still worked wonders, knew I was no

7

longer a leader of the yippies. Remember the Liddy plan to kidnap "radical leaders" and hold them in Mexico during the 1972 conventions? It was part of the master plan that included bugging the Watergate headquarters of the Democratic Party. In his book, *An American Life, One Man's Road to Watergate,* Jeb Stuart Magruder writes about the Liddy proposal:

> The mugging squads, he [Liddy] explained, could rough up hostile demonstrators. The kidnapping squads could seize radical leaders—he mentioned Jerry Rubin and Abbie Hoffman—and hold them in a "safe house" in Mexico during the Republican Convention.

I wish Liddy had kidnapped me. Instead of trashing me, the kids might have started a FIND RUBIN movement.

It isn't enough to learn lessons in the abstract. For me to grow personally, Ruthie had to leave; and to accept the fact that I was no longer a youth leader at thirty-four, I had to get kicked in the behind. In truth, I had become more conservative; aging had mellowed me. I didn't feel old but I was no longer young. After the conspiracy trial in Chicago I thought my life would never again be as exciting. After writing *Do It!,* I felt that I could never again write anything as effective. I was competing with myself, and living in the past, looking backward rather than forward.

My friends were battered, too; "punch-drunk" is the way John Lennon put it. It wasn't the FBI, CIA, or Pentagon that scored this victory over the "leaders of the left." We were eaten for breakfast by our own. When we in the movement realized we weren't going to dismantle the system, we turned our hostility against each other. In 1969 the movement began to amass real power, and we began to criticize each other, more effectively than the repressive society ever did. We feared success.

The movement destroyed its leaders. It may have been a necessary destruction since we were out of touch with our people, but it was done in anger, not love. The method of attack contributed to the disappearance of the movement as a moral force. By 1972, I was a battered soldier who hated his ego, feared his power, and was contemptuous of his name. Pain had become my teacher.

One day in December, 1974, I was eating pita bread and humus in a restaurant in the West Village with some friends. Lennie Weinglass looked up and asked me, "Do you think there is such a thing as *male* menopause?" Lennie was one of my lawyers during the Chicago trial. During the days of police confrontations, we were too busy making history to devote much time to self-indulgent activities such as friendship. Like the society we opposed, we directed so much of our energy outward into achievement and manipulation that we had little time left for anything else.

In the 1960's I would have laughed at the idea of male menopause, but now my mind ticked off all my male friends in their thirties. A few continued with enthusiasm, but many were experiencing the common symptoms of depression, low energy, and loss of ambition. What had caused it? The aging process? The disappointing way the sixties had ended? The difficulty of being a male in this society?

My mind flashed back to a poignant moment in another Village restaurant four years earlier with Tito

Gerassi, a fiery revolutionary writer who knew Che, Huey, Eldridge, and Fidel. Like me, Tito believed that he was a self-sacrificing guerrilla struggling to bring freedom to the world. But his eyes were sad. The movement's energy was petering out and people were spending more time attacking each other than attacking the state. Tito looked at me and said, "I have finally accepted the fact that I am never going to be a Che Guevara." I felt sad when I heard Tito say that. Even at *that* moment I still saw myself as a Che.

I needed one more disappointment to teach me that the movement of the sixties was over and that I needed to change. I had always dreamed that some major rock superstar, like Dylan or the Beatles, would join the movement and help galvanize young people politically. In 1971, I saw a photograph in the New York *Daily News* of John Lennon and Yoko Ono arriving in New York. I called them, we met one afternoon in Washington Square Park, and then began hanging out together during the next few months.

I felt that yippie was Beatles' music put to politics, and John was the most politically aware of the Beatles. In his *Working Class Hero* album, John was singing to my soul. I found him to be a good friend, honest, loving, and brilliant. Yoko surprised me the most. She had been portrayed as responsible for the breakup of the Beatles, the Oriental woman who had stolen our man, our music, our youth. I did not appreciate the depths of sexism and anti-Japanese prejudice until I met Yoko and discovered her soft and gentle soul. She is one of the dearest and smartest human beings I've ever met. Open about her pain and her pleasures, she has a Zen-like way of looking at the world.

Immediately, the three of us began fantasizing. We would launch a musical-political caravan, tour the United States, raise money to feed the poor and free prisoners from jail. The shows would combine music and fun with political education and consciousness-raising, and all the money would go to the people!

I came often to visit them at their bed. In those days John and Yoko slept, ate, wrote, and conducted business from an enormous king-size bed in their apartment in the West Village. With them I discovered the utter absurdity of fame: they could not go anywhere for fear of being mobbed. Crowds huddled around John as he walked down the streets, and he had to brush people away. Waitresses got so nervous, they would drop their dishes.

All the potential paranoias of human interaction are exaggerated by fame. Sometimes I looked at them and all I could see was the myth. I would think to myself: Oh wow, how exciting, I'm with John Lennon, I want to hold your hand! Then I would look at him again and see a scared, bright, working-class kid with granny glasses. I could see the person behind the image and I would feel genuine love for him.

John was very interested in politics, and for months I brought scores of revolutionary political figures of the sixties to their bedside for animated discussion: Abbie Hoffman, Dave Dellinger, Huey Newton, Bobby Seale, Rennie Davis. One night, four of us—Abbie, myself, John, and Yoko—took a knife and cut our fingers and smeared the blood together in a blood oath "for the hell of it" on the front page of Ram Dass's book, *Be Here Now.*

John and Yoko suggested that I join their fledgling

band (even though I could neither carry a tune or play an instrument) to break my isolation as a politico out of touch with the music. So John handed me a drum, and asked me to help play back-up on "Imagine." The next week the band played at the Apollo Theater at an Attica benefit, and I was there with a tambourine. When John and Yoko hosted the "Mike Douglas Show," I helped them back up Chuck Berry doing "School Days." This, the culmination of every musical fantasy I'd ever had, was possible only because every musician had sound amplification but me.

The first stop on our political-musical tour was Ann Arbor, where John Sinclair, chairman of the White Panthers, had been sentenced in 1968 to ten years in jail for possession of two marijuana joints. John and Yoko agreed to appear at a rally to pressure the Michigan Appeals Court to release Sinclair, who had already spent two and a half years in prison. Music and politics combined to fill the stadium on December 10, 1971, with fifteen thousand people and win headlines across the state. The speakers were Bobby Seale, Rennie Davis, Dave Dellinger, the Reverend John Groppi, and me; the music was provided by David Peel, Stevie Wonder, and John and Yoko. Sinclair talked to the rally from a telephone in jail, and when he described the conditions there, the crowd seethed with tension. Two days later the Appeals Court released Sinclair from prison, a stunning victory for the merger of music and politics.

At the same time, however, Attorney General John Mitchell ordered the Department of Immigration to begin deportation proceedings against John Lennon. Mitchell was worried about the political effect of our tour on Nixon's re-election. The government used an old marijuana bust of John's in England as a technicality to begin the hearings. The threat of deportation forced John to cancel concert plans and concentrate his energy on the fight to remain in the United States.

As the government closed in on John, he got paranoid; for a time he even considered the possibility that I was a CIA agent who had snuggled close, seduced them into a rock tour, and then nabbed them. He didn't really mean it, but the hot breath of the U.S. government complicated our friendship.

I learned a lot from John. As an ex-Beatle he received as much pleasure as an ego can sustain in money and mass love. Yet he was unsatisfied. Backslapping from the outside was not what counted. What counted was how John felt about himself. His post-Beatles music and his private life exemplified this desire to know himself from the inside out.

John eased me over my age hurdle by telling me how proud he was to be thirty-one, "The best age of all." And I remembered reading somewhere, "If you're unwilling to grow old, you are unwilling to grow up."

Chapter 2
Searching for Myself

I MOVED from New York to San Francisco in November, 1972. New York is a city for the ego, a media orgone box where people relate to each other as images. I wanted to free myself from the tyranny of time, but in New York every second counts. The clock is king, and its symbol is the clicking meter in taxicabs. I wanted to move, temporarily, at least, from a state of doing to a state of being, but in New York the first question people ask each other is, "What do you *do?*" That same question is an insult in the Bay Area, where nobody does anything. Instead, the question is, "What are you into?" and the answers are likely to be yoga, modern dance, hypnosis, and woodcarving.

Besides, maybe something new was cooking on the West Coast. From the beatniks and hippies and antiwar activists to the Patty Hearst kidnapping and the grass-roots explosion in body awareness and spiritual consciousness, the Bay Area seems to give people permission to experiment, go crazy, try something new. Then the ideas get packaged by the media in New York, and are sent as myths to the rest of the country, where the real germination takes place.

Ahhhhh, San Francisco. So many nights in Japanese hot baths, so much time spent getting massaged. Soft, quiet, feminine. So much time to do nothing. I felt the magic of San Francisco, city of hills: a place to reflect, grow, enjoy; the scene of spiritual Renaissance.

But I found people on individual trips barely communicating with each other. In such a fairyland environment, personal relations tend to be breezy and nonintense. People need each other in New York. When you reach someone's house, get inside the double locks, escaping from the cold of February or the heat of August, you sigh, "I made it, I wasn't mugged, I'm so happy to be here." Every person on the streets of New York is a type. The city is one big theater where everyone is on display.

San Franciscans struck me as bland. The empty psychic spaces made me nervous. I felt edgy, as if I was missing something. I found myself resenting the provincial pride of these people: they see themselves as the center of the world. Cross the bridge to Marin County and one suffocates with specialness. Mention

New York or—perish the thought—Los Angeles to someone in San Francisco, and prepare for verbal vomit. In San Francisco everybody is supposed to be high and happy, the reverse of New York, where cynicism is the secret language.

What I missed most in San Francisco was Jewish soul. San Francisco is a WASP town. Even its Jews don't act like Jews. I longed for an intellectual New York Jewish friend almost as much as chicken soup. I craved New York's intensity and high-powered energy. San Francisco turned out to be granola for my mind: nutritious but uninspiring. Instead of watching the evening news, I was watching the sunset.

Mellow was the word for San Francisco. The silence drove me out of my mind and deeper into myself. And that's what I had come for—to rediscover my body and spirit.

Much of my life I've spent running away from myself. It was time to look at myself in the mirror, stay there and be myself, or die. It's easier never to stay in one spot—run, avoid, move, be very busy doing nothing.

I've searched the whole world for something *out there* to give me pleasure *in here*. When I thought I had found the "perfect woman," she held a mirror up to my face, forcing me to see myself more closely. When I run, I'm relatively happy, looking for tomorrow's diversion. But there are no diversions against the self.

There were many things I refused to see in the sixties because I hid behind the radical leader image; my personal life was at the service of a public existence.

As long as I had an investment in being Jerry Rubin the image I could not grow. I had to free myself from my self-image, my public image; I had to kill Jerry Rubin to become me.

The moral drive that inspired me in the 1960's never left, although the media described me as going from politics to a preoccupation with my personal life. I was called a "health food nut" by the *National Lampoon.* During a newspaper interview I told the reporter I had just finished jogging. "Jogging?" he asked. "Have you gone Establishment?"

In the movement of the sixties we were guilty of many of the things we were fighting against in America. We were male chauvinists, we competed, we were entranced by the mystique of violence, we glorified youth, we lost touch with our bodies, we oversimplified reality, we became images to each other while playing the theater of protest. We OD'd on our own energy, demonstrated, screamed, pushed ourselves to exhaustion, and needed a rest to catch our breath. We lost control of our own energy. We manipulated ourselves into premature confrontations with men who used guns and brute force. We needed to stop—and look. It is vital for us to go inward and see how similar we are to the society and the parents against whom we are protesting. Changes cannot be made on the political level alone, or the society we are changing will be repeated. We must examine our own process.

The movement of the sixties was a wave of history that made its splash and settled into the restless waters. Instead of being *the* movement, we have become part of the flow. More waves and flows are to follow.

The excesses of every decade are corrected by the

17

excesses of the next decade. Each decade rejects the previous one to establish its own identity. Today, the 1960's radical movement is sometimes dismissed as a flapper period, a period of extremism and craziness. The scary thing about the end of the sixties is that many leaders of the movement have committed "suicide." When I became aware of this tendency of symbolic figures to self-destruct once their public identities fell apart, I knew I would have to change radically to survive.

I used to scorn therapy as psychiatric escapism, yet here I was in 1974 dedicated to my own self-therapy. I berated Eastern spirituality in the activist 1960's, yet in 1973 I was bowing to an Indian swami and spending my time reading Eastern philosophy. I said "kill your parents" in 1968 and "love your parents" in 1974.

This happened to thousands of people at the beginning of the seventies. "We are the first generation to reincarnate ourselves in our own lifetime," a friend said to me. A communist friend of the sixties has become reincarnated in 1975 as a ballet dancer and poker player. Ex-radicals and ex-revolutionaries meet these days in farms, gestalt groups, therapy retreats, meditation sessions, and welfare lines.

The phone rang. It was Rennie Davis. He had just returned from India and his voice was as high-spirited as if he were announcing the next peace march.

"God has returned to the planet, Jerry," he said to me. I humored him, but he pressed on.

"God is on the planet in a human body," he said. "And I've met him!"

While Rennie talked, I recalled the night he, Tom Hayden, Abbie Hoffman, Dave Dellinger, and I were

found guilty and jailed on a five-year sentence climaxing the conspiracy trial in Chicago. We had all criss-
crossed the country giving speeches prior to our jailing,
and as we lay in our bunks that first night we could
hear the television in the main room announcing that
students on many campuses were protesting our imprisonment.

Rennie shouted, "Rioting in Madison! That's me! I
did that one!" Abbie bellowed with joy at the announcement of rioting in Boston. I listened for the names of
schools where I had rabble-roused. It was happening
everywhere. A few days later, the five of us sat around
wondering what might happen to us over the next
five years. We all expected to die, or go underground
and assume new identities, or remain in prison. No one
even suggested that the movement might slip away.

Now, as Rennie talked on and on about finding God,
I remembered our conversation in jail, and a feeling of
the absurdity of life swept through me.

My journey into myself is not a unique journey. For
the past few years a new consciousness movement has
appeared in America: there are yoga classes, meditation groups, sex-therapy clinics, spiritual movements,
change-yourself consciousness courses like est (Erhard
Seminars Training), women's consciousness groups,
increased interest in preventive medicine and body
awareness, and a new passion for honesty that resulted
politically in Watergate.

America is going through massive self-examination
on the individual level. That inward-look is quietly and
nonviolently transforming the values and attitudes of
the middle class. Millions of people have begun to look

deeply at our own lives, bodies, social relationships, life purpose.

Finding out who I really was was done in typical Jerry Rubin way. I tried everything, jumped around like crazy with boundless energy and curiosity. I lived in an atmosphere of personal growth, and absorbed its values with my Woody Allen way of tripping over my own passion.

In five years, from 1971 to 1975, I directly experienced est, gestalt therapy, bioenergetics, rolfing, massage, jogging, health foods, tai chi, Esalen, hypnotism, modern dance, meditation, Silva Mind Control, Arica, acupuncture, sex therapy, Reichian therapy, and More House—a smorgasbord course in New Consciousness. I'd be up at 7 A.M. to jog two miles, then run from modern dance class to tai chi practice to yoga to swimming to an organic meal to a massage class to a sauna bath to a night therapy or growth group, with weekends filled with more growth and spiritual activities.

I entered the consciousness movement in search of my body, my sexuality, my health, my spirit. I discovered that I had not made peace with my parents. In 1974, at the age of thirty-six, I needed to take a new look at myself as a little boy. How much of this little boy is still in me? How much of my parents? I needed to go on a self-discovery journey to free myself from my past.

I went through a three-month process called psychic therapy, which helps free people of childhood programming by working out love-hate conflicts with parents. After doing the therapy, I freed myself from rebellion against my parents.

I went into therapy for growth. Not fully in touch

with my own feelings and needs, I was closed to myself, and therefore closed to others. I felt nervous and lonely. I felt that if I could *see* myself I would *love* myself.

This is my story—with its pain, breakdowns, anxiety, breakthroughs, and growth. It is not a finished story. By the time the story is written, I will be in a different place, evolving further. My venture into everything from bioenergetics to yoga to psychic therapy was a kind of theater, a new form of having fun with myself, a game, like taking a walk on the beach, hitchhiking around the world, raising a child, cooking a meal. The best thing I can do for myself is look in the mirror and laugh. The more seriously I take myself, the funnier I am. It's all a joke. *"Who cares?* What's the difference?" In that absurd spirit, my journey begins.

Chapter 3

Am I My Stomach or My Tongue?

EVERY time I move into a yoga position, such as the shoulder stand, some part of my unconscious recalls the image of my mother dying of cancer at fifty-one. For two years, I went to the hospital every day and sat next to her bed, doing my college homework.

To the end she believed she had hepatitis and would recover, even though she kept getting weaker and losing weight; pound by pound, death ate her up. Her pain was so great that I found myself praying for her to die.

"Why is life so mean?" she would say. Then one day

she died in my arms. "Bye, Mother," I said. "I'm sorry."
The next year my father was fighting for breath in an oxygen tank. He was forty-nine, full of energy, spirit, drive; but he had had five heart attacks in three years, and now he was dying. The only treatment his doctor offered him over those years was pills, and postattack rushes to the oxygen tank.

My father was emotionally upset at the time and needed some sort of psychiatric help. A healthy society might have saved him by providing a more supportive environment; instead, he was left to die.

To the doctor, my father was just another patient. "Look, Jerry, of course your father needs psychiatric help, but he can't afford it. If he goes to a psychiatrist, he will kill himself worrying about how he is going to get the money to pay for it." Money to pay for it! My father is going to die because we can't afford to save his life. Western medicine had nothing to offer my father. Call it a heart attack, but he really died of the loneliness, isolation, fear, and competitive pressures that marked his environment, and the total absence of anything that would encourage positive health.

What a backward medical philosophy! Competitive life in America creates diseases and then doctors charge exorbitant fees to cure symptoms through surgery and pills. I had spent two and a half years visiting my dying parents in hospitals and was appalled at the impersonal way they were treated by nurses, doctors, and the entire hospital bureaucracy. I considered their killers—cancer and heart attack—"social" diseases. I promised myself not to die that way.

But in the 1960's I ignored my body, eating fast

23

foods, taking drugs, forgetting to sleep. As Hal Jacobs once said, "You guys tried to give your body away in the 1960's. Now you are doing everything you can to get it back." My body felt like a sack of potatoes; I weighed 160 pounds and people called me chubby.

In examining my life, I began with my body. I was killing it with poor food and air. I had been programmed to equate growing old with suffering and disintegration. But I am my body. Everything I do to my body is reflected in how my body feels. I am what I eat. I kept a weekly record of the things I stuffed myself with: the sweets, rich foods, and bread that I love. My body became my teacher. My body moves at its own pace and knows its limits. I began to listen to all parts of it and to exercise.

For a few years I cut out meat, sweets, and carbohydrates, after conversations with a nonmedical healer, Jack Soltanoff. I ate fruit, vegetables, fish, and chicken. Slowly, my sense of my body began to change. I felt in touch with my digestive process. I needed to sleep less. I lost thirty pounds and looked and felt lean and trim.

I entered the world of health food through Adelle Davis. She had me eating hamburgers for breakfast, followed by thirty vitamin pills. After every meal, I'd take out my pills and begin gulping them down. I can't really say I felt any better, but I trusted Adelle Davis. Then she died of cancer. . . . I still take daily vitamins, even though my medical doctor tells me all they do is give me expensive urine.

I love the thick taste of carrot juice. I feel it hit my blood stream at first swallow. So healthy, like drinking Nature itself. Then one day during a checkup my doctor gaped at my legs and said, "You've turned orange—do you drink a lot of carrot juice?" I looked, and sure enough, my legs were orange. My doctor assured me there was no harm in the condition as long as I didn't mind orange legs. Not taking any chances, I cut out the carrot juice.

I started reading and following nutritionist J. Rodale until he died of a heart attack on Dick Cavett's national television show in the midst of explaining how good nutrition guarantees a long life.

All this was leading me to preventive medicine: the body as an energy system. The food we feed it is energy. Blocks slow down the energy. Tension is blocked energy. That tension enabled me to lead demonstrations against the System in the sixties. Now I want to learn to relax my tension, so that I can be active in a more relaxed, centered way—not to avoid tense situations, but to relax my systematic body tension.

My entire body is a living organism in a constant process of construction and destruction. Disease is breakdown, not an external invasion. The emphasis in preventive medicine is on breathing, on stimulating acupuncture meridian points for energy, relaxation, and exercise. I fancied becoming an unlicensed doctor of positive health, serving people yoga and vitamin pills; offering pulse diagnosis and foot massages; prescribing jogging, meditation, and natural herbs. For a time I considered opening a health-food restaurant called "Jerry's." Retired radical hangs around to discuss radical politics and internal health around the juice bar.

My love affair with positive health was not without

its lighter moments. When the acupuncture craze hit America, I was an early adherent. I heard of a man I'll call Dr. Fong in Riverdale, California, and I called him for an appointment. He balanced my body energy ("chi"), by sticking little needles in me. I felt great. I convinced my friend Rhoda to go for treatments.

The weird thing about Dr. Fong is that he's an alcoholic. He drinks whiskey steadily during the day and keeps a bottle on his desk to fortify himself before inserting the needles in you.

He looked into Rhoda's eyes, felt her pulse, and told her that she had cancer in both breasts. I gulped; tears welled in my eyes. Only thirty-four and cancer in both breasts! "Oh, Rhoda," I said sadly. But Dr. Fong moved to reassure her. "Don't worry, dear, because I will cure you with one acupuncture treatment." I heaved a sigh of relief. Rhoda looked at us as if we were both loony, but as she said later, "I knew that I wasn't going to get out of there until both these men saw needles stuck in me."

Dr. Fong inserted fifteen needles from her ears down to her toes, twisted them around, and abruptly pronounced Rhoda cured of cancer. We left, I feeling contrite, Rhoda shaking her head. But before we left, Dr. Fong sold me a special supply of 200-year-old licorice-tasting ginseng cubes, which I was to take three times a day for continued energy balance and long life. Acupuncture has its positive points, but after that experience I never returned to the good doctor, even though I know he's a great acupuncturist.

Then there was the day my chiropractor on the West Coast told me I had hardening of the arteries and high blood pressure. The chiropractor said he could cure me through regular adjustments, a vegetarian diet, and metabolic slowdown. I agreed and threw myself into his health program, determined to cure myself.

Months later I discovered that I never had either hardening of the arteries or high blood pressure. Was my chiropractor a kook? Or was he frightening me into positive health? Does it make any difference?

Some people say all emotional problems are the result of vitamin deficiencies. Others advocate an all-grain diet. Health-food people debate the merits of milk. Most people, however, agree that sugar is bad. How can you believe all the theories of preventive medicine? Everybody says his thing will cure everything, from the reflexologists who see the key to health in the feet, to those who advocate the many versions of miracle diets.

I entered the new health area with the same save-myself, save-the-world fantasies I rode in the political movement, looking for a new myth, a new collective way. Anyone with alluring bait got me on his hook.

If everyone would get rolfed the world would be saved!

If everyone meditated there would be no more war!

In fact, I've got the answer to all the world's problems: wheat germ!

Medical doctors strike me as ignorant as to how a *healthy* body works. They know how to control or repair some diseased bodies, but their medicine is often worse than the disease. And what about the pressure and competitiveness of the pharmaceutical industry and the make-profits-quick motives of the food corporations? Medical doctors put little or no emphasis on nutrition, exercise, and energy balance. They are paid when we are sick, not when we are well. The new health consciousness of the seventies places the emphasis on health rather than disease.

I reached my mid-thirties afraid of overtaxing myself physically. Then I met fifty-year-old men who ran eight miles a day. I thought about Dick Gregory, who fasts a lot, eats only fruit, and runs fifteen miles a day. I began jogging.

What fun! At first I couldn't jog half a block without running out of breath and feeling my legs screaming in pain. But gradually I pushed on until I was running three miles a day. The outpour of sweat and rush of blood through my body kept my energy high all day.

Jogging got me in touch with my mind-body blocks, but I find it very hard to start. My mind produces a million good reasons why *not* to take that first step. As soon as I take the first step, I get going for a while and my mind relaxes. Then after a short while I come to another crisis. My mind tries to tell me that I am tired. It whispers, "We have important things to do, you've run long enough." At first I fell for these lines, but then I realized that my mind was speaking instead of my legs. When I listened to my legs, they said, "Yes! Keep going." If I anticipate this resistance point, I can recognize it and quickly go beyond it. My mind learns that it is not the undisputed czar of my body.

My mind must have something to do. As in meditation I make up a mantra to keep my mind occupied so that my thoughts won't interfere with my experience. I repeat the mantra over and over; my thoughts pass by me, without my getting stuck on them.

If I fight them, they stick.

I have to be aware of other tricks of the mind. My mind loves to impose impossible demands on my body. "You must do more. You are stopping too soon. Other people do better than that." I must resist this do-more, do-better propaganda campaign. Overdoing is a basic characteristic of my psychological armor. I think I am not enough, so I try to do more. I learn to be unattached to these thoughts. When my body says stop, I stop.

I also began to look at the world within. One day I saw someone doing yoga and joined in. Pretty soon I was going every day to the yoga institute. At first I could hardly bend. My body was tight, blocked. But the yoga attitude toward change melted my resistance: you begin exactly where you are and move from there. No competition, no straining, no trying, no striving. Every move counts, every stretch stretches. I felt myself looser and looser.

I went on a ten-day yoga retreat in upstate New York. We meditated, did hatha-yoga, heard lectures on calming one's inner desires, and maintained absolute silence. The silence experience was a first for me. Most of my life I have directed my awareness outside of myself. I felt it was time to go inward and make contact with my lost center. I found it hard to take the silence experience completely seriously, however. One afternoon I slipped away from the retreat to drive to town, read a newspaper, eat some chocolate, and make an orgy of phone calls to friends in New York.

Then I met Swami Raj-ji. He was a living example of the power of yoga, an eighty-year-old man with the body of a fifteen-year-old: he could twist himself into an unbelievable pretzel. Rich folks met him in

Paris and brought him to an Upper West Side apartment in New York to teach yoga. I was invited to meet the little white-bearded man with the penetrating eyes, and I began doing yoga with him every day. He looked at me with his clear, beautiful eyes and said, "Happy?" I looked back, "Yes, happy."

In this era of gurus, it was appropriate that I would find my own. When I confided to Rennie Davis that I'd met Swami Raj-ji, he warned me that the media might use it: "Yippie Leader Finds Indian Swami, Drops Out of Politics." Ironically, two months later Rennie declared his public obeisance to Guru Maharaj Ji.

I didn't like Swami Raj-ji's attitude toward politics: meditate and all the world's problems will go away, he said. That struck me as a gross simplification. We began arguing. "Meditation hasn't solved India's poverty problems," I said.

For the next month I worked with Swami Raj-ji forty-five minutes every day. He quickly saw what parts of my body needed loosening and led me through a series of exercises that left me feeling stronger, happier, refreshed. I thought to myself: How lucky I am. My own personal Indian swami, one of the hatha yoga champs of India, and now he's all mine!

As the exhilaration wore off, I couldn't help noticing some strange things about Swami Raj-ji. He wanted me to write a book with him, to become his disciple and promote him. He told me that Swami Satchdanada was a fraud. "He's nothing back in India," Raj-ji said. "He had to come here to be accepted."

I couldn't figure out whether he was satirizing an ego or if he really had one. Was he an Indian master playing the ego game in America, or was he just holding a mirror up to me? As he continued putting down all the other gurus, however, I realized he really was an egomaniac. He wanted followers. Well, I guess that's the Indian swami dream: come to America, renounce the world, and get rich. What difference does it make? He is a fine yoga teacher.

I turned my friends on to the swami, starting with a married couple. He saw the husband alone for a half hour. "You need to be celibate for a while," Swami told him. "Too much sex is bad for your energy balance." Then Swami stayed an hour and a half teaching yoga to the wife. "You need more sex, more orgasms, more energy in bed," he told her, and offered to see her every day.

Didn't he think they'd compare notes?

I brought another woman to see Swami Raj-ji. After telling her to do yoga in the nude, he began massaging her body. Then he invited her to take a shower with him. He said, "I will give you divine orgasms." She said no thank you and excused herself. She asked me what the hell did I think I was doing sending her to an eighty-year-old Indian sex nut?

I discovered that an Indian swami is just as human as you and me. Swami Raj-ji demonstrated he could control his heartbeat and claimed to be above desires. But he turned out to be as funny and crazy as everyone else. My respect for Swami Raj-ji rose after that realization. He's the best yoga teacher I've ever met. He claims he sleeps less than two hours a night. One morning while I had my legs over my head in the plough and I thought I was keeping the position for an extra long time, I looked up and saw Swami

Raj-ji asleep. I laughed, and came out of the pose on my own.

I wanted to learn from Swami, not become his disciple. One way that people are discovering themselves in the seventies is by surrendering to a guru. The disciple gives up personal blocks and allows the guru to remold him. The surrender speeds the transformation by eliminating all resistance.

Many people get in a high space and go through many changes through surrender. As long as people can go in and out of that space, it's positive. We all surrender to something—our work, lovers, beliefs, creations. A life without surrender is a life without commitment. But I'm too rebellious; I can surrender for a while, then I rebel.

I separate the physical exercises of yoga from the religious connotation. Yoga is fantastic training for the body. It stretches the inner organs, something Western calisthenics ignores, and promotes positive health by constant communication between mind and body. Yoga stimulates blood flow and deep breathing which postpones physical degeneration—and disease. It conditions the body, mellows the emotions, uplifts the spirit, slows down the organism. It's something I'd like to do every day for the rest of my life.

When I am depressed, I find my way out of my depression by taking care of my body. When my body feels good, I feel good. The food I eat and the exercises I do determine my mental and emotional state. In yoga I slow down my breathing, concentrate myself into different postures. By slowing down my metabolism, I calm my mind. Stretching my body automatically relaxes my mind. By relaxing my body, I attack my emotional imbalances. A nervous body creates a nervous mind. After yoga I learned to control my wandering thoughts for the benefit of my entire being.

As I sit in a yoga position and watch my thoughts pass by, I realize that I am not my thoughts. Thoughts, scary, positive, or weird ones, pass through my consciousness all day and night. I can pick and choose the thoughts that I want to be me; the same is true about feelings.

Yoga got me in touch with the "me" beyond my thoughts and feelings by slowing me down enough so that I could watch myself the way an outside observer might. That impartial observer within me is me laughing at all my "important" struggles. That objectivity—or freedom from myself—is true freedom; it is the goal of the spiritual path.

During the 1960's I had only occasional flashes of this spiritual feeling. Most of the time I was satisfied. As long as I was getting satisfaction from my attachments, I had no desire to experience nonattachment. To get in touch with the yoga of nonattachment, I had to lose what I had.

The "outside witness" feeling rarely stays with me; it comes and goes. When it's not there, I become my desires. If my desires are not satisfied, I am not satisfied. When I am attached to yoga, I can be unattached to other things.

Through the body revolution we are discovering a human potential we never before imagined. We can control our nervous system through our breathing. My mind, by tuning out outside distractions and listening to the world within, can harmonize with my breathing like a machine; it can actually hear all the parts of my body function.

By their lives my parents told me that being sick is better than being healthy. Our society teaches us that profits are a higher priority than health. Every day now I am choosing to break my parental and the societal prohibition against being healthy; I am giving myself permission to be healthy.

At the age of thirty-seven I feel like twenty-five, because for the past five years I have eaten healthy foods, jogged, done yoga, taken sauna baths, visited chiropractors, gone to acupuncturists. I am beginning to make my body my best friend.

Chapter 4

Naked on the Couch

Y OGA is good for the body and the mind, but even after three hours of peaceful yoga my emotions can drive me crazy. Will I die like my father, a failure of the heart? He suffered one of his heart attacks during intercourse, and I have used this as an inhibition on myself. Watch out, do not lose control, hold on, you may die making love!

Laying spirituality and philosophy on top of my emotions is like laying shit upon shit. I've attended scores of "personal growth" workshops and learned all about losing my ego and dropping my attachments. I agree, feel good, am enlightened! Then the minute a crisis appears, the insights disappear and the devil in me takes over. I become that six-year-old Jerry who screams, cries, complains, and manipulates when he does not get his way. The intellect is but a speck on the ocean of emotion.

Yoga and other forms of meditation do not deal directly with emotional problems. Rather, meditation directs the consciousness into a calm place, curing "neurosis" by a sophisticated form of repression called "maintaining internal peace." The peace gradually forms a mental habit and dissolves unsolved childhood conflicts.

The practice of yoga is evolving, though, and many people are mixing Eastern mind control with Western psychological release. While I plan to maintain inner serenity by daily yoga, I also feel the need to meet my emotions directly. Too many people do yoga sitting on a repressed emotional tinderbox, trying to solve emotional imbalances with spiritual diversion. Spirituality flows out of clear emotional feeling.

As a verbal artist, I knew that "talk" therapy would not be as effective for me as direct work on my body. So I looked for therapies that promised radical transformations of the body and discovered rolfing, bioenergetics, and Reichian therapy.

What I heard about rolfing scared the shit out of me: some sadist pulls, punches, and squeezes you while you scream and cry and hurt your way to heaven; you lay naked on a bed and a rolfer pounds the pain out of your body. I dared myself to try it.

The theory behind rolfing is that as we grow, we

store our unhappy emotional experiences in different parts of the body in the form of muscle tension and rigidity of connective tissue. This blocks energy flow and keeps us from realizing our energy potential.

Rolfing, named after its eighty-year-old founder, Ida Rolf, is usually a ten-session experience at about thirty-five dollars a session, and is designed to renovate your entire body. A rolfer uses his elbow, fists, hands, and the weight of his entire body to move into areas of blocked energy and to soften emotionally traumatized tissues by physical manipulation. The release of long-held tension frees us from internal suffocation. Each session the rolfer concentrates on crushing a different part of your anatomy.

I made an appointment to see Michael Salveson in Oakland. I was scared. Did I really have to go through all this pain to free my body of its hang-ups and tension? Michael asked me to undress and then he took a Polaroid picture of me. I lay down and he started to work on me. I felt him press his fists deep into my groin. If I fought his hands, the pain was greater, so I decided to ride the pain as if it were a wave in the ocean, rather than to resist it. He pressed for three seconds, then released. I felt "ahhh" when he released.

I allowed my mind to aid his fist, picturing the area he was working on as sand that he was driving through. Surprisingly, the pain was not as bad as I had been warned it would be. Pain is a physical sensation, like pleasure, and I learned that if I can get into the sensation itself, concepts like "good" and "bad" and "pain" and "pleasure" have less meaning.

I remembered walking in the freezing cold of New

Jerry Rubin

York one day while on acid. The cold felt like a sensation, neither comfortable nor uncomfortable. I felt detached from the pain. I thought to myself, "So this is what cold feels like." In rolfing I experienced that same awareness of pain as a neutral sensation.

In subsequent sessions the pain was so great that at times I asked Michael to stop. And, immediately, he would. The most painful parts of my body were my feet, legs, and heels, and then the pelvis. I liked it when, after pummeling me, Michael would lovingly return to massage the area with light strokes.

At the end of each session he took another picture of me and compared it to the one he had taken before. My legs seemed straighter, my shoulders less rounded. My pelvis was beginning to relax out, rather than in. My weight felt more evenly distributed.

In the sixth session Michael pushed his hand through my stomach from the front, moved around the intestines and reached the other end. As I lay there I saw his hand go right through my body! One false move . . . Seconds later he slowly moved his hand out. I had to respect the rolfer's ability to know where everything is.

The eighth session, which I had heard about for weeks in advance, was the most challenging one. It's called the nose job. Michael sticks his finger up your nose almost into your forehead to break up the tense cavities. Well, if other people had survived, I would too.

Sure enough, as soon as I arrived Michael put on his rubber glove. He put his finger up, up, up—wouldn't he ever stop? How far could he go? He was going to break my nose!

It was either panic or submit.

I gave in, allowing Michael to do whatever he wanted. He did the second nostril. And then, unsatisfied, he repeated it in both nostrils. By that time I was deep into the Eastern concept of letting go. The moment I gave Michael full control over my body the nose job felt good.

After ten rolfing sessions my body weight was stabilized at 130 pounds. My spine felt straight, my body more relaxed. I felt looser, less tense, and more in touch with my insides. Michael told me to come back in nine months for four hours of tune-up.

Rolfing, of course, does not perform miracles. How do I reverse thirty-six years of conditioning in ten hours? If the memories are still there, won't the tension accumulate again? And if I don't continue to practice relaxing parts of my body, won't the old patterns re-form?

My parents sent me to a shrink when I was sixteen. All he did was take notes while I fidgeted and tapped my fingers impatiently. In the 1960's I saw therapy as adjusting people to a sick system. Social revolution was the only effective therapy. I attacked psychiatrists, pitied people who went to shrinks, and condemned the self-indulgence of paying thirty-five dollars an hour to hear that you are fucked-up because of what your mother did to you at age four.

Yet here I was in 1972 about to drop that same amount of money an hour to see a bioenergetic therapist who works on blocks that prevent a free flow of body feeling and energy. I was in the therapy room of Stanley Goldman, a 250-pound roly-poly Jewish Daddy.

Jerry Rubin

Bioenergetics is a body therapy, descended from Wilhelm Reich through Alexander Lowen, which is based on the theory that breathing blocks curtail energy.

As soon as I came in, Stanley asked me to undress to remove the protection of clothes. Then he asked me to move my feet. I began running, kicking, bicycling in place. Stanley pointed out my main character armor: chest out, shoulders tense and stiff, a protective, resistant posture to the world. "Relax your chest, let your shoulders down, let your stomach out and down, live in your belly, Jerry," Stanley said. "Breathe in your abdomen. There's a real struggle going on between your chest and your abdomen. You're a nice Jewish boy and you've been told not to breathe in your abdomen. You are rebellious on the outside, but on the inside you are conservative, you repress yourself!

"Jerry, you are going to die someday, so be yourself! Let yourself be foolish!" Stanley was screaming.

As a child and teen-ager I felt angry, hostile, and rebellious toward my parents. My body language said, "keep away." I developed body blocks as protections against pain and feeling. But what was functional for me as a child does not serve me as an adult. I no longer need those body blocks. Stanley and a host of other body experts are creating an internal revolution by putting people in touch with natural body feeling.

I also went to a Reichian off and on, a white-haired gentleman whom I'll call Tim, in his mid-sixties, with a reddish complexion, a heavy-set appearance, and a fatherly tone. Reichian therapy is breathing therapy. There is little talk. I stripped naked and fell on my back on Tim's king-size bed. "How's the man?" he asks. "Good." "Really?" "Well, not so good, the same." I closed my eyes and Tim told me to breathe heavily in and out. I felt the armor across my lower chest blocking my energy. As I breathed I felt faint, about to lose control. My mind switched to what I was going to do the rest of the day. I began to feel dizzy. "STAY WITH THE FEELING, JERRY," Tim yelled.

My mind wanted to take me away from my body. My head felt light, as if it was falling away. "Good, your head has too much control usually," Tim said.

My hands and my fingers were vibrating with painful sensations. Pain flowed through my lower body and legs. I wanted the pain to stop, the session to stop. Tim compared my situation to a person recovering from frostbite. At first there is no sensation. Then there is pain. The pain is positive, restoring feeling. Eventually the feeling of pain evolves into pleasure.

I put my knees up on the bed breathing in and out. Every few minutes Tim took my pulse. He pushed in on my stomach. He breathed heavily in and out, and I tried to imitate him and his sounds. I brought my mind back to my body. I was impatient.

The sensation in my hands and legs from the heavy breathing was pleasurable. He pressed on my eyes, mouth, face. Tim suggested that I take up hobbies like swimming or dancing. "Get out of yourself. Be good to yourself. Have fun. Forget your problems," Tim said.

I went to Tim for about ten sessions, but when he

41

hiked the price from thirty-five to fifty dollars an hour, I quit because I couldn't afford it any more. I also resented his attempt to cut off everything relating to my personal growth beyond his therapy.

Therapists need to establish their authority over you. It's part of transference theory. The therapist, in becoming your new daddy, begins to undo the negative programming you got as a child. Daddy and mommy said no and you have internalized your parents by saying no to yourself. The therapist says yes, to feelings, to pleasure, to enjoying your body; yes to doing whatever you have always wanted but feared to do.

You give your therapist a lot of power over your life. The therapist's response will have a powerful effect because you have opened yourself up and are vulnerable and undefended.

Reichian work broke down my psychic and physical inhibitions and put me in touch with primal drives, but its philosophy was disturbingly conservative. Tim's views of men and women reflected standard male chauvinist thinking. The women's role was to have children and take care of the home. Monogamy was the only way to achieve a healthy sexual life.

I advocate growth programs in which you take an active part in your own growth, and your friends become your therapists. I prefer therapeutic communities, or therapists who are part of your daily life. What is needed is a mass transformation of the body energy of society. For example, Reichian work and bioenergetics to supplement coffee breaks in factories; body camps for people in the city; state-subsidized people teaching each other about relaxing and enjoying the body, a mass exchange of techniques and skills; a free yoga class in every neighborhood.

The body revolution cannot take place within a therapeutic framework. Who can spend thirty-five to fifty dollars an hour to undo breathing blocks? These forms of therapy are unconscious holdovers from Freud, and fit in with a capitalist system in which you sell and buy services. Therapy is becoming Big Business, the "service trade of the 1970's," as *New York* magazine put it.

Stanley helped me to *feel* my insides. But in the end, I rebelled against his authority over me in the therapeutic situation. I dislike the basic psychotherapeutic system of going one hour a week to a shrink, paying bread, ending when the clock says it's over. Seeing your therapist can become an addiction.

Both Stanley and Tim told me that changes would take years, and they made the process very mysterious. They perpetuated the medical myth that the doctor is responsible for your health. Both said: Do nothing else but come to me once a week and forget about yourself the rest of the week. They had little or no advice about preventive medicine, exercise, or diet.

In the new therapies, the therapists often spend a lot of time attacking each other. Stanley thought every other therapy was negative or harmful. He made fun of gestalt therapy; he even criticized other bioenergetic therapists. Tim told me that meditation is bad for you because it takes the energy away from your sexual chakra and puts it in your head. He also warned me that jogging creates body rigidity, and that yoga curtails body energy. Since I wanted to sample many different experiences in the growth area, to find the ones most sympathetic to me, I felt very uncomfortable with their "me-or-else" attitude, an attitude that unfortunately was very prevalent in the growth movement.

Chapter 5

Meeting the Female in Me

I WAS already in the growth movement, but my anxiety over Rhoda sent me in deeper. I wanted to find out what was going on inside me and to make the relationship work. I felt dependent, lonely, and scared, and through the various growth experiences I hoped to discover the roots of my dependence on Rhoda.

Meeting Rhoda dispelled my conviction that there would never be another woman for me after Ruthie. Now I felt that there would never be another for me like Rhoda. I was "in love"—but I didn't feel good. Love was supposed to bring happiness, satisfaction, contentment; instead, it brought me pain. No matter how much love I received, it was never enough. I kept wanting more. When I felt loved, there came the panic: what if I lose it?

People had told me a lot about Rhoda: they said we looked alike and had similar auras. Rhoda was a well-known gestalt therapist in San Francisco and I was interested in learning about gestalt therapy. So I called her up and told her I wanted to meet her. We got together in a North Beach Italian restaurant and discovered we had known each other all our lives even though we had never actually met before. I had finally found the woman I was searching for: a woman who was interested in people and social change, who was powerful yet soft; a warm, short, dark-haired, bouncy woman with piercing eyes, sensuous lips; a thirty-four-year-old Jewish woman from Brooklyn who was charting her own course in life, with a certain tough-mindedness that hooked me. Being a romantic, I did *fall* in love. But in falling in love with Rhoda, I was falling in love with myself. Rhoda was, as I told a friend later, a "female Jerry Rubin." Is it any surprise that I was holding her hands fifteen minutes after meeting her, and before the night was over, I was asking her to marry me, have children, write books together, and form a unit against the world?

I believe in monogamy and prefer an intimate, committed relationship with one woman to a series of scattered involvements. Beneath my radical ideology of independence and freedom is my desire to marry a supportive and loving woman, raise a family, live in the country, and grow vegetables.

I packed my suitcases and arrived at Rhoda's house and we began to live together. Rhoda's physical presence sent an energy rush through my entire body. With her I learned some very beautiful things about myself: that I am able to give myself to another person and share my deepest feelings. I fell in love with her love for me. I saw my love reflected in her eyes when she looked at me.

Yet, as Rhoda herself told me the first day we met, and practically every day thereafter, my description has nothing to do with her! I saw My Dream and made her My Dream. When two people come together, they produce two relationships. What I am describing here is only my experience, my relationship, not Rhoda's.

For the next two years, Rhoda and I loved like crazy and fought like crazy. We ran like children through the streets of San Francisco and traveled together to Jamaica, Haiti, Paris, London, and Ibiza. We dreamed big dreams. We met every important person and visited every place in each other's past lives. We became inseparable, and I began to lose my identity in love.

The consciousness changes of our time affected our relationship. Rhoda and I dramatized the male-female war. In many ways we switched roles. Having made it "as a man" in the 1960's, having won fame and power, I wanted to settle down. I felt no need to make my mark on the world again. I found myself saying things traditionally associated with women. I even thought, maybe I would stay home and raise the baby, wash the dishes, scrub the floor, and change the sheets while Rhoda went out to change and influence the world. Rhoda, however, felt a need to create, accom-

47

plish, express herself. I wanted to marry. She replied, "Why bring the government into our relationship? I thought you were supposed to be a revolutionary."

My involvement with Rhoda brought all my ambivalences to the fore. I wanted to live with her, possess her. I thought that unless we were committed to each other, the relationship could not grow. Rhoda had her own ambivalences. As a liberated woman, she wanted her freedom, including the freedom to see other men. I felt jealous. She felt smothered. At the same time, I picked up Rhoda's repressed desires to marry, have children, raise a family, be an adoring wife to a protective husband.

With Rhoda, I saw how heavy it is for a woman to reach her mid-thirties without having a child. So many women today are struggling with their identities as women and the question of whether one needs a husband and child to be a woman. I felt that conflict within Rhoda, and within myself. Like many childless people in their mid- and late-thirties, I experience baby panic.

I tell myself: "To be a man I must be a father. I am getting on in years. What if I never have a kid? What will I be missing?" Sometimes I feel an almost biological desire to have a child.

But as a child I saw my family as a prison. My parents told me how to think and what to be. I looked at my father and mother and vowed not to repeat their dull lives. I developed a strong ego life outside the house. This has resulted in my living all over the country, escaping rather than staying in one place with a few people and accepting the possibility of boredom and prison. Now I want what I missed and I feel cut off. It makes me uptight to hear that someone has children. The older the kids and the younger the parents, the more jealous I get. Yet people in family situations tell me they envy my freedom and opportunity to make an impact on the world. We all seem to want what we don't have.

But the truth is that I am not ready to become a prisoner to an infant. Even though I might play at getting in touch with the housewife within me, I was not ready then to give up running around to become a father.

I am thankful to the women's consciousness movement for widening the choices for me as a man. I can not marry or have children and still feel good because the social definition of adulthood has changed in the past ten years. While I am grateful for the choice, I am still not free of the inner dilemma. Part of me feels worthless if I do not have a child. Is that part the internalized voices of my parents and relatives, whom I am trying to please? Or am I responding to a true biological statement? I don't know.

With Rhoda I experienced all my inner dilemmas, and it hurt to feel such conflicts. I wanted a family with Rhoda, but at the same time I thought we should have an open, liberated relationship.

Rhoda and I saw a union between my yippie politics and her gestalt therapy. Yippie is gestalt theater of the streets, compelling people by example to change their awareness. Entering a Congressional hearing room in a Paul Revere costume or wearing judicial robes to a court proceeding is a way of acting out fantasies and ending repressions. In the sixties, we were doing gestalt therapy on the nation, helping people discover their inner strengths and take responsibility. Our actions provided a model of freedom and as theatrical therapists we used the media to help turn a nation of sheep into rebels and activists.

Rhoda was also doing yippie therapy, helping people connect to their inner strength. Gestalt therapy is a yippie theater of the psyche. The individual acts out his forbidden thoughts, and actually becomes his fears and fantasies. If you're having a conflict with your mother, you resolve the conflict by taking the role of your mother and experiencing both parts in a theater-of-the-absurd.

I attended one of Rhoda's groups as a silent observer. Some of the group members requested that I leave because they said my presence changed the group. I refused to leave; they sat and complained about my being there. Rhoda said, "If you want him to leave, do something about it." Four people jumped up and began to carry me out. At the door I said, in a voice just above a whisper, "Isn't anybody going to help me?" Suddenly the room exploded, and for the next fifteen minutes thirty people pulled me in and out of the room, tearing my clothes, wrestling with each other, acting out their impulses. Gestalt is "do it!" therapy.

Rhoda and I had differences here, too. I thought gestalt therapy focused too much on the individual and not enough on society. The goal of gestalt therapy, individual awareness, seemed insufficient; I believed that only collective action, through collective awareness, could create liberation. Rhoda felt that if we brought people to a healthy acceptance of themselves as loving beings, the system would naturally become healthy and loving.

I said, "It is impossible to become a healthy and

loving person in an unhealthy and unloving system. Only political action can change the system."

Rhoda said, "It takes healthy and loving people to create healthy, loving political action."

We became the yin and yang of psychology and politics. Eventually we rapped ourselves into a synthesis, and soon Rhoda began sounding like a political revolutionary and I like a psychological freedom-fighter. We switched roles.

It reminded me of my relationship with Abbie. At first I was the political internationalist and Abbie the fun-first hippie. After a while, though, Abbie became the political heavy, and I became the know-yourself-first dropout. Then we switched back again. With people who influence each other, sometimes it is hard to know where one begins and another ends.

Like me, Rhoda is a performer and loves to rap before crowds. We began doing workshops at Esalen, giving speeches and holding press conferences together. Outside attention put additional pressure on our relationship. Rhoda felt overwhelmed by my fame.

At a consciousness festival in San Francisco Rhoda and I spoke together. We threw balls of white bread at the audience to signify the emptiness of American food, and passed out healthy bread for people to taste; we smoked joints and passed them around. We spoke of the need to combine internal and external change. Rhoda talked passionately, yet the next day the San Francisco *Examiner* published only my picture, with no mention of Rhoda. I had specifically asked the reporter covering the story, a woman, not to let that happen. Afterward, she said that the copy editor had cut Rhoda out of the picture and the story. The tendency of the media to cover only people who are already famous, especially men, hurt our relationship. It reminded me of the political movement of the 1960's when comrades did things with me and then read in the paper that they were "Rubin's lieutenant" or "Rubin's girl friend."

My fame was a problem, almost like a third person on the scene. I sometimes forget that I am two people, me and my image. Then something happens that I do not understand until I remember that I'm never alone. I've got an image right here and that's what people are reacting to.

Rhoda and I planned to organize huge events together. We developed the idea of Body Day, a consciousness festival to be held in Golden Gate Park: twenty thousand naked people massaging each other on national television, ten thousand people doing yoga together, eating natural food, doing tai chi, rolfing, and acupuncture—the merger of the inner and outer revolutions. We broke up, however, before the event was organized.

We both treasured our individual freedom more than the relationship. Adventures in the outside world were more important than creating a harmonious home together. For several months we tried living together, but each of us felt our freedom was being curtailed by that arrangement. As two strong people, we began to compete. When we went through one of our regular breakups I felt empty, scared, powerless. I moved into my own apartment.

Rhoda refused to make a commitment to me because she was keeping to her gestalt philosophy of living in the moment. Commitments imply dependency. She was with me today, but tomorrow was another day.

Still, the gestalt concept of living in the moment was therapy for me. My parents instilled in me a deep expectation of living for the future. Go to high school so you can go to college. Do well in college so you can graduate and get a good job. Work six days a week so you can rest on the seventh. Work so you can retire in old age. Live morally so you go to heaven. Everything is put off until tomorrow. But there was one secret my folks never let me in on: tomorrow never comes. When tomorrow comes, it is today.

Gestalt therapy says that you take responsibility for everything that happens to you. The moment you say, "I couldn't help it, some crazy feeling came over me," you are abdicating your own power and becoming helpless. In the middle of a fight Rhoda would say to me, "Jerry, take responsibility for that feeling." Yet during a heated argument, that tactic becomes a power move, especially if you get into the Catch-22 tricks of self-awareness. By telling me to take responsibility, Rhoda herself was giving up her own responsibility.

I introduced Rhoda to my radical comrade of the sixties, Stew Albert, at his Upper West Side apartment in New York. Stew argued that despite heart trouble he could never give up his anger because it represented his rebellion against injustice in the world. Rhoda said that his anger was causing him tension, and not helping to end injustice in the world. She suggested that he beat a pillow with Nixon's name on it to work out his anger. "I'm too much of a Marxist to do that," Stew said. "I know Nixon is not the pillow."

"O.K.," said Rhoda, "then chop wood."

Stew had high blood pressure and an irregular heartbeat, and medical doctors put him on pills. He forgot

Rhoda's gestalt suggestion to chop wood. But three months later Stew and Judy Gumbo decided to move to the Woodstock woods to a house heated only by a wood-burning stove. The fierce Eastern winter drove Stew to chop wood three hours a day to keep warm. The move to the country and the wood-chopping lowered his blood pressure, and his heartbeat returned to normal. One day he threw his pills over the mountainside. A victory for gestalt therapy over Western medicine!

All relationships have a power aspect. I gave away my power to Rhoda, and I don't know why. Never before had I been in a relationship where I felt powerless. I wanted a traditional relationship with Rhoda—and I felt my feelings were "bourgeois," "old-fashioned," "old consciousness." So I accepted her view of the "right relationship"—with its openness, distance, freedom, and self-responsibility—and ignored my own needs.

Yet the relationship had such value for me that I couldn't break it. We learned positively from each other. On a deep level we loved each other. We became sources of strength for each other, mirrors of each other's inner beauty and outer strength.

If we had been able to make it, it would have been a powerful union. The excitement of the challenge intrigued me. I was hooked; Rhoda became my addiction.

Even though she was a therapist, and I was deep into various therapies, we were not beyond the games all people play in that scary adventure called intimacy.

RHODA: I want you.
JERRY: You have me.
RHODA: Then I don't want you anymore.

"Whenever we get angry, we're really hurt. Let's tell each other immediately by saying 'ouch.'"

RHODA: Ouch!
JERRY: Ouch!
RHODA: Ouch!
JERRY: My ouch is bigger than your ouch!

By loving Rhoda, I was attached to her; I could not live without my love for her. By needing her, I had a stake in her being a certain way. When Ruthie left me in 1970, I tried to hold her by telling her how much I *loved* her. "Your love," she replied, "oppresses me."

I fear aloneness, and think I need a woman to keep me warm. Oh, how lonely it is to go to sleep and wake up alone in bed. How secure knowing that every night Rhoda and I would have supper together, that if I wanted to go to a movie she would be my companion, that I always had someone I could discuss my innermost secrets with. But then why did I pick a woman who I felt rejected me? Did I love the rejection too? Was Rhoda bringing out my self-rejection? Was I replaying some tape I learned in childhood?

Later, while doing psychic therapy, I learned that with Rhoda I had unconsciously reproduced many of the same reject-me games my father played with my mother. That insight helped free me from my attachment to Rhoda.

My search through the therapy wilderness was in one sense an attempt to make myself acceptable to Rhoda. Rhoda became my reason, but reasons are irrelevant. I created Rhoda as my excuse to do trips that brought out my essence, my own soul.

In doing psychic therapy, I exorcised my parents.

Would the same work for an ex-lover? With Rhoda I experienced the pain of separation. As long as I blamed myself for the failures in the relationship, and felt "I was not good enough" or "if only I had done something differently," I was stuck in self-pity. By taking Rhoda off the pedestal, seeing her as she was, I freed myself.

But blaming Rhoda kept me attached to her. I was angry at her because I still wanted something from her. Anger is as strong a bond as love. I then forgave Rhoda and loved her for being exactly as she was. Rhoda was Rhoda. I put my awareness on the positive experiences for both of us.

Friendship is my model for love. In many ways love is an obsessive-compulsive attachment to another being: "I cannot live without you." More pain goes down in the name of love than any other human emotion. I have treated my friends with more care than I have often treated people I was in love with. I do not expect my friends to be a certain way, but I have huge expectations about my lovers.

The couples that survive are the ones who are friends on the deepest level. Love is a firecracker that goes on and off. Friendship nourishes, feeds, and endures.

I no longer believe that my life will be a failure if I do not succeed in romance and coupling. If I match with someone on my journey, beautiful. If not, my life will still be complete and my journey valid.

A lover is like an addiction. Giving up the addiction is harder than giving up the person. My lifelong search is to learn to love myself enough so that I do not need another to make me happy. As I come to that place of self-love, I am able to love another.

A friend remarked to me the other day that he was searching for the "perfect woman." I told him that the perfect woman already exists—inside him. Love is not finding the right person. Love is being the right person.

My relationship with Rhoda and my experience in therapy helped me accept, love, and develop the female side of me. With Rhoda I became conscious of my yin-double, the woman-inside-of-me. I was chasing her, never catching her. And of course, through it all I knew who Rhoda was. Rhoda was me. Rhoda was the me-inside-me that I had created to prove myself to me.

Chapter 6

The Making of a Dissident

I am five years old and walking down the street with my grandmother. I want an ice cream cone. My grandmother says no, supper will be soon and I'll spoil my appetite. I start screaming and crying. I run into the middle of the street, fall down on the trolley car tracks, and hold on to them, screaming. "I'm not going to get up until I get ice cream!" Grandmother tries in vain to pull me off. It finally takes two men pulling and tugging to get me off the tracks. My civil disobedience career begins early in my life. I don't remember whether or not I got the ice cream.

But I got everything else I wanted as a kid. I was spoiled, an only child until the age of nine. Even then my parents told me that they had Gil because I seemed so lonely.

There had been too much tension in the home for me to feel loved. My parents met while on separate vacations in Miami Beach and, five days after meeting, were engaged to marry. My mother was my grandfather's special pet, his only daughter; she had been babied since birth. When she brought my father home to Cincinnati, her family did not like him. They considered him a gruff New Yorker without manners, not good enough for my mother. "Why is Esther, an honors college graduate, marrying this bum—who quit high school at fifteen?" My mother's four brothers were so hostile to my father that they took him for a ride and roughed him up. My father would feel rejected by his in-laws for the rest of his life. Not long before his death, he cried to me about it.

I am now aware of a huge rejection button right in the middle of my forehead. It's pushed all the time and I feel rejected, even when I'm not. I'll even reject others so they won't reject me. Now that I realize I picked this up from my father, I can ask myself: "Am I really being rejected or is my rejection button just being pushed?"

The child in us keeps trying to win daddy's love by being just like him, even when it causes us physical and psychological pain. I seized the inner self-image of the rejected one to be like my Big Daddy. Inside, my father was, no doubt, just a little boy playing out what he had learned as a child from his Big Daddy.

My mother was an exceptional woman who lived an unexceptional life. She graduated from high school and college with honors, then worked as a nurse's aide; she played classical music on the piano with skill and read books constantly. She might have been a teacher or writer; her upbringing, however, conditioned her to be a housewife. When she married my father and gave birth to me, she relinquished her independence and became a full-time housewife.

Mother spent twenty years attending to my every whim. If I sniffled, she was right at my side. She made my bed for me the second I got out of it. She picked up my underwear off the floor. She refused to take vacations for fear of leaving me alone. I resented this attention and pitied my mother for having to stay at home all day with nothing to do but gossip on the telephone or shop at the supermarket. Mother accepted as her role making life easier for the men around her.

Mother taught me compassion. People always mentioned her consideration for others. Outwardly, I rebelled against that consideration, but inwardly I knew she was right. Her entire being radiated sweetness; she was unable to express overt hostility to anybody.

My mother saw herself as a person sacrificing for others. Her mother, my grandmother, suffered a crippling stroke when I was twelve. Mother persuaded my father and me, against our wishes, to live in the same house with her parents for six years, so we could take care of them. I grew to hate the responsibility of having to take care of sick grandparents.

Mother could not handle my rebellious behavior. Instead of thanking her for taking care of me, I condemned her. I saw her care for me as service, not love. She had a difficult time expressing affection and rarely kissed or touched me. She repressed herself and shared her internal existence with no one. She got anxiety attacks in supermarkets and always had to sit in aisle seats in movie theaters. She had many obsessive habits, like washing her hands fifteen times a day. When she finally died of cancer, I remember thinking, "She brought it on herself. She had a cancer personality." I hated myself for thinking those thoughts.

My father was a high school dropout who never read a book. He drove a bread truck for fourteen years to support the family. As a young kid I was ashamed of him. Unlike the other Jews who had moved into suburban areas to escape the invasion of black people, we had to stay in the old neighborhood. Every Sunday my uncles came over to my grandfather's house, where we lived on the second floor, to tell jokes and stories. The stories always dealt with how they made money. They were competing for my grandfather's attention, but my father either sat in the corner saying little or retreated upstairs. He wasn't as verbally acute as they were, and in their opinion, he was just a schlemiel from New York.

My father ran away from family rejection by making his mark on the world. He started a booster club and succeeded in bringing professional hockey to Cincinnati. When I was a kid playing softball for the Jewish Center, he became manager of my team and coached us to the championship. When I became a Cub Scout, he became my pack's leader. At the same time, he was busy from 3 A.M. to noon every day delivering bread.

When I was in my mid-teens my father went through a transformation as he became more involved in the activities of his union local. Every afternoon he was on the phone: "Hi Emil, I'm Bob Rubin and I'm running for business agent of the union. I'd like your vote. I think that I can represent you well." I listened with admiration as my father, without embarrassment, called worker after worker and won the election. Suddenly he had an office, a new car, a secretary, and a cause to inspire his life. I was proud of my father.

I got my first taste of political activism while my father was the bread union leader. Early in 1955 he organized a strike of bread drivers to fight for a five-day work week. For two months, the bread drivers fought on while the owners refused to budge. Media pressure called for an end to the strike. Finally, Jimmy Hoffa flew into Cincinnati and told the drivers to call off the strike because it couldn't be won at that moment. Daddy disagreed, but went along with Hoffa on the promise that a coordinated national truckers' strike would help win future strikes. During this time, Hoffa was being investigated by Congressional committees. My father became a strong Hoffa supporter, calling him a powerful fighter for working people. He told me that America feared the strength of the working class.

My parents thus communicated to me a very traditional male-female role model: passive mother, aggressive father. I absorbed my mother's internal soul and my father's external nature, bringing the two extremes together within my own synthesis. My shyness and my exhibitionism reflect that dual nature. I withdraw like my quiet mother; I project like my boisterous father.

I always thought I was the opposite of my parents. I rebelled against them publicly, seeing the hypocrisy in my own family reflected in society as a whole. After the sixties ended and I got into the growth movement, I discovered that though I rebelled against my parents,

I had in fact reproduced their psychic structures inside me. By copying my father's external energy and my mother's internal fears, I had duplicated their lives.

At home at an early age I intuitively grasped the hypocrisy of class distinctions. We had a black maid. My father called her Pepsi because she drank so many glasses of Pepsi-Cola every day. When my mother got sick with cancer, Pepsi came every day to cook and care for Gil, who was then six years old. Although she got paid very little money, she developed a real love for our family.

Pepsi was always smiling, keeping us laughing during those dark days. After mother died, she began taking care of Gil. Because of Pepsi I began to think about the injustice of American racism. All my friends had black maids who came once a week. I felt there was something wrong with a society that taught its black kids to be maids.

To this day Gil and I keep in touch with Pepsi. I visited her in 1973 when I went to Cincinnati and she greeted me with a ten-minute hug and tears. "I love you and Gil as much as I love my own children," Pepsi said.

In Cincinnati, white Jewish people didn't like blacks. At first, most Jews lived in Avondale. Then a middle-class black family bought a house in the neighborhood. The whites in the area tried to block the sale because "it brings the value of the neighborhood down," and "once you let one in, they all want to move in." Within a few years Avondale was half-black. The wealthier whites escaped into the white suburbs farther out and were replaced by blacks. In school, blacks and whites stayed in separate areas.

I began to identify with blacks and defend them in

family discussions. The more I defended them, the more emotional the arguments got and the more convinced I became that I was right. I noticed the gap between my parents and our relatives. They made more money and put us down, while also attacking blacks. As a young kid I said to myself, "I'll show them." Twenty years later, as a radical on campus attacking the war and capitalism, I thought to myself, "I did show them."

I lost my political virginity at the age of fourteen in 1952, when I saw Governor Adlai Stevenson on TV welcoming the Democratic Convention to Chicago. I fell in love with Stevenson's humor and idealism, and for the next six months I worked for his election. When he lost to General Eisenhower in a landslide, I was heartbroken. At that moment I think I may have unconsciously decided to become a radical. Something *was* wrong with the world, and I was going to fix it.

I felt inferior to the wealthier Jews in Cincinnati who lived in all-white suburbs and went to all-white schools. They were being groomed for Eastern colleges and careers as doctors, lawyers, and businessmen. The son of a truck driver, I was stuck in an inferior school. My dream was to get into Walnut Hills High, an elite school that took only those kids who passed a special city-wide test. I failed the test in the seventh grade, but tried again in the ninth grade and I got in. But, once there, I felt excluded from the social circles of kids who had known each other for ten years. They had the right smiles, the right clothes, the right parents, the right manners. I felt I had to prove myself to them and I deeply resented them.

Yet I had enormous self-confidence. I proved myself

to them as my father had proved himself to my uncles, aunts, and grandfather. The first year I joined the school newspaper. The way to popularity in school was through sports. I couldn't play worth a shit, but I soon became famous as the sports writer who decided which players' names would make the paper. As a freshman I was interviewing famous seniors, who recognized my power as a writer. I was making it; I knew all the "big men" in school.

The most important quality at Walnut Hills was good looks. Ugly girls had it particularly rough. I thought to myself that if I were an ugly girl, I would consider killing myself. This tyranny of beauty drove us crazy. All we cared about was our appearance, our image, our clothes, our friends, what other people thought of us. Nobody ever taught us to care about what we thought of ourselves. It was always: what do *they* think of *me*?

I had a complex about being short, 5 feet 5½ inches. I wasn't as good as the taller boys, and the girls didn't like me. Yet because I was short I tried harder and achieved more; inside I often felt like a superman whose energy could turn the world upside down. To cure my own unhappiness at being small, I got interested in ideas, like the meaning and purpose of life. Even though I made the best Jewish fraternity in school, I still felt inferior. A high school friend recently said, "The guy in our school who was least likely to be Jerry Rubin was Jerry Rubin."

I couldn't identify with the small, ostracized group of intellectuals who read philosophy books, had communist ideas, and were despised by the majority of kids. I thought that they were weird. Although I re-

65

belled against the values of the "in crowd," I wanted to impress them. I was a C student. I was scared of girls and did not date much. While other boys went across the river to Newport, Kentucky, to whorehouses, I threw all my energy into journalism and became sports editor of the *Chatterbox*. I convinced myself that with drive and purpose I could do anything in life.

Before graduating from high school, I made contacts with sports reporters at the local daily, the Cincinnati *Post and Times Star*. I started off compiling statistics for high school sports, then I got a summer job running errands between the newspaper and the race track. It was my first job. I got my first byline in the paper at the age of seventeen, and today, twenty years later, I still find it hard to describe that incredible feeling I had when my articles appeared. I kept reading my article, looking at my name in the paper, and knowing everyone would see it.

For the next five years, I worked on the newspaper staff, making my way up the ladder. I worked sixty hours a week and also carried a full load of American history courses at the University of Cincinnati. I wore white shirts and bow ties to work. For a while I was a feature writer for the paper, interviewing major league baseball players, like Ted Kluszewski and Roberto Clemente. One night I went to Dayton with the entertainment editor of the paper, to see a raw young comedian named Lenny Bruce. I fell in love with Lenny and went to see him again the following night. Someday, I told myself, I would be like Lenny Bruce, speaking out the truth about our society.

Within a year, I was named editor of my own two-page youth section, with my picture and byline in the

Post every week. I had reporters in every high school and college in the city. I covered proms, high school clean-up and patriotism campaigns, writing stories on the prettiest girls and the best school citizens. The editor of the paper used to tell me how proud he was. "You're going to be a great newspaperman someday, Rubin," he said, seeing his own reflection in my eyes. (What an embarrassment it must have been to him eight years later when I reappeared in the pages of his own paper as a shaggy-haired, dope-smoking "dangerous radical.")

At first, I loved working on the paper so much that my pay checks would gather dust in the financial office until the clerk brought a fistful of them to me. The other reporters looked at me resentfully. The union leader complained to me because on my vacation to New York, I spent my time interviewing Pat Boone, Dick Clark, Fabian, and Frankie Avalon, and working longer hours than the other reporters.

One day it all stopped being fun. I used to have lunch with reporters twenty-five years my senior. All told the same stories of how the bright dreams of their youth had been drowned in Scotch and despair. Was this going to be me? To advance I knew that I would have to kiss ass and sell soul, and even then the boss's son would by-pass me.

I concluded that the paper would be healthier if all the workers from reporters to truck drivers owned the paper, made decisions collectively, and distributed the money equally. When I suggested that idea to several reporters, they started calling me a communist. This was 1957 and at first I was very insulted. "Communist! How dare you!" I said, storming away.

Jerry Rubin

I spent most of the day trying to convince people on the staff that I was right. At the same time I protected myself with my little boy smile so that even though people felt frustrated by me, they still thought I was cute. I was preparing myself for yippie politics. Were we hard-core, dangerous revolutionaries or cute goof-offs? Nobody could pin us down, and that was our survival loophole. The moment we got described as violent traitors, we reappeared as good Jewish boys. The moment we were accepted as good Jewish boys, we turned again into obnoxious radicals.

My experience on the paper ended my desire to make it within the channels of American society. I still wanted to make it, but I no longer knew how. One day as I was thinking about quitting the paper, even though I was making top salary, I was listening to Buddy Holly sing "Peggy Sue" on the car radio. I heard a news flash: "In Berkeley, California, students are battling police in protest of the House Committee on Un-American Activities!" It was May 13, 1960; I was twenty-one, lost and confused, bored at being a newspaperman. There was a more direct way if you wanted to be near news: Berkeley! It would take me five years to get there, but the minute I heard that radio report I decided I would go to Berkeley and help create events that would become radio headlines in between Chuck Berry and Elvis Presley, headlines that would inspire other people like me locked up in the prison of no-choice. From there on in, I only had to acquire the self-confidence to get there.

My mother's cancer had first been diagnosed in 1954 when I was sixteen. She had three operations and doctors felt that they had saved her. Five years later she developed pains in her gut. For a year and a half she was in and out of hospitals, and finally in the summer of 1960 she died.

Nine months later I bought a plane ticket to Lucknow, India, where I could live as close as possible to the India-China border. India was the wave of the future, and I decided to go there to study politics. I was going by myself to a place where I would not know a soul. I packed up all my belongings and left my brother and father, who had already had five heart attacks.

But while sitting in a youth hostel in Berlin, ready to go to the airport to fly to India, I heard my name announced. For the past three days American Embassy officials in three countries—England, France, and Germany—had been making an exhaustive search for an American whose father had died four days earlier in Cincinnati, Ohio. My father keeled over and died of a broken heart, just eleven months after my mother had died, while I was tripping around Europe. I thought of my brother Gil left without parents at the age of thirteen and started crying. I turned in my Germany-India ticket and returned to Cincinnati. I arrived too late for the funeral. My father, not quite fifty, was gone.

I wanted to live with Gil, care for him, watch him grow, love him. I became his legal guardian. One part of me said, "Good, now that my parents are dead, I can really teach Gil the truth about life. I'll raise the perfect son, and be the perfect parent." I moved into the room where my father had died a month earlier and mother had battled cancer for five years. It was not a time for rejoicing. But I got pleasure from the belief that someday I would be a great philosopher and teach the world the truth. I pretended to read books from morning to night—philosophy, psychology, novels. I got to page twenty in every book, stopped and moved on.

My desire to go to India remained. When my aunts and uncles heard that I planned to take Gil with me, they intervened, threatening to go to court to prevent me from taking him there. "There are tigers in the streets of India," one uncle said to me. "That's no place to take a small boy." Under their pressure I gradually decided that it wasn't worth it. Instead, after seeing *Exodus,* we changed our minds and decided to go to Israel. I told our relatives and they were overjoyed. Tigers did not roam the streets of Tel Aviv.

Gil and I packed everything we owned into six huge trunks and we took a boat to Israel. We were not going there to settle, but anything was possible. From afar, Israel looked like a country where Jews from all over the world were cooperating to create a socialist society of love. I engaged a number of Arab foreign students in Cincinnati in discussion and felt that their arguments against Israel were right, but that didn't bother me. I'd go to Israel and convince the Israelis of the rightness of the Arab cause. Like Ghandi, I would convince the Israelis to offer love to the Arabs.

Gil and I arrived in Jerusalem where we found an apartment three blocks from the Knesset, the Israeli Congress. I enrolled as a graduate student in sociology at Hebrew University; Gil began studying Hebrew. For the first time in my life I felt what every American feels when he goes to a foreign country: impatient at the noise and dirt, contemptuous of people who do not speak English. I was a true-blue chauvinistic white middle-class American. I hated this part of me and began seeking out people at the university who shared my idealism.

I introduced myself to a bespectacled, thin, light-haired Israeli who fascinated me with his disarming smile and determined expression. I told him I was an American studying sociology. His answer almost knocked me off my seat.

"I'm a Communist," he said.

Never before had I heard anyone say that he was a Communist so matter of factly, like he was telling me it's a sunny day. Another new friend was an Israeli whose father held a high position in the government. One day he called me into a corner of the library and told me that we could not hang out together any more. He needed a security clearance to get a job in the diplomatic corps and an agent of the Israeli government had warned him that I was an American Communist who was spending time with "Arabs and Communists" in Israel.

I walked home that night in the brisk Jerusalem air with my heart pounding. Me a Communist? Who was watching me? The only political thing I'd ever done in my life was hand out anti-fallout-shelter leaflets in Cincinnati. Me an enemy of the government? Even though I did have some Communist ideas, I felt myself very loyal to America. Yet someone in the Israeli government was watching me. Little me, a danger to the Israeli government! I was proud and scared at the same time.

The Israelis wanted the very things I was escaping from: material goods. "How much does that cost?" was the question they asked me most often. They were fascinated with my huge tape recorder and pile of tapes of American rock 'n' roll music. My stay in Israel turned to disillusionment. I saw Jews from the Arab world mistreated and dominated. Israelis openly described Arabs the way whites talked about blacks in America.

I respected the Israelis as people, but I felt frustrated whenever politics came up. The very things I was running away from in America I found in Israel. My heart was Jewish but my head leaned toward internationalism.

After six months of living with me in downtown Jerusalem, Gil moved to a kibbutz, where he lived for a year. During that time he went from boyhood to manhood. He learned Hebrew and worked in the fields developing his body. Israel matured my brother and radicalized me. After a year and a half in Israel, Gil and I decided to return to America—to go to Berkeley. On the way home we stopped in England and heard that earlier that day President Kennedy had been assassinated.

Chapter 7
Life as a Sixties Radical

arrived in Berkeley in January, 1964, at the age of twenty-six, with short hair, a handlebar moustache, white shirts, and sports jackets with holes in the sleeves. Within two weeks I had met every radical in town. I ran from group to group asking a million questions about politics and the movement, putting it all down in my notebook. Some people thought I was a cop.

One day a woman asked me to go with her to a picket line protesting a local grocery store which discriminated against hiring black people. I recoiled. "That's showing off, getting attention for yourself," I said. Even though I considered myself a Marxist, I was an uptight, scared college intellectual who had not yet smoked dope. But I went anyway, and that first picket line changed my life. I loved fighting for causes I believed in, and meeting women at the same time.

After six weeks of attending courses at the university as a graduate student in sociology, I quit to become a full-time picket-line walker. I walked in more circles than anyone in town.

I heard that a radical organizer was in town looking for eighty volunteers to go on an illegal, free trip to Cuba. That struck my fancy. If the government didn't want us to go, there must be something to see. Since travel to the island was outlawed, we had to go the ninety mile trip from Florida to Cuba via a most circuitous route. We flew to Paris, where we got a plane to Czechoslovakia, where we boarded Cubana Airlines to fly back across the Atlantic to Havana—thirteen thousand miles to go ninety miles! When the plane landed in Cuba, all eighty of us cheered: "We've arrived in the Free World!" We had outsmarted the CIA and made it to Cuba.

Cuba transformed my consciousness. I saw with my own eyes how the victims of American imperialism had translated abstract dreams into reality. The fancy hotels in Havana, once gambling casinos and prostitution havens for American businessmen, had been turned into schools and homes for the poor. Students graduating from medical school went to the hinterlands to serve the peasants. The entire society was putting into practice the Christian ideal of fellowship. Why then was America determined to destroy the Cuban revolution? Cuba had set a "bad boy" example for the rest of South America. Washington resented Cuba's break away from being a plantation economy serving American corporate interests. Cuba had to be smashed.

We listened to Fidel Castro speak for seven hours to 200,000 people. Then, a few weeks later, he and the Cuban cabinet played a ten-inning baseball game with American newspapermen who were visiting Cuba for the first time in years. Fidel pitched Cuba to a 26-2 victory, giving America a message in terms it could understand. What a yippie Fidel was!

I looked at the Cuban people and envied their revolutionary spirit, their enthusiasm and aliveness. I wanted to stay and live there. The Cubans said, "No, your struggle is in America." We interviewed Che Guevara, the Minister of Labor, who was already secretly planning to leave Cuba to spread the revolution elsewhere. He blew my mind when he told us that if he had a choice, he would return to North America with us. "The most exciting struggle in the world is going on in North America. You live," Che said, "in the belly of the beast." Inspired by Che, I returned to the United States. At the border the U.S. government revoked my passport.

A month after I returned, the Free Speech Movement broke out on the Berkeley campus. The huge FSM student demonstrations reminded me of Cuban rallies, and Mario Savio reminded me of Fidel. The issue in the FSM was the right of students to plan on campus illegal civil-rights activity that would be held off campus. The deeper issue was the nature of power and education in the university; students were, as Mario put it, being molded rather than educated. I attended every FSM rally, meeting, and activity. I listened, watched, and got my training. The FSM climaxed when thousands of Oakland police invaded the campus to make mass arrests of students who had closed down the administration building with a sit-in. A successful strike followed the police arrest and closed the university. Students had won the battle.

Inspired by the FSM, a group of us organized "Vietnam Day," a nonstop thirty-six-hour marathon teach-in which drew twenty thousand students to listen to Senator Ernest Gruening, Dick Gregory, Phil Ochs, Norman Mailer, Isaac Deutscher, and I. F. Stone. It was an incredible event with songs, speeches, debates, and an empty chair signifying the State Department's refusal to attend. After the teach-in everybody asked: "What next?"

Berkeley is near Oakland, the military shipping point for Vietnam. Trains passed through Berkeley carrying soldiers to the Oakland Army Terminal. Our next dramatic move in the antiwar theater would be to block the trains. It was a surreal scene: cops chased the kids off the tracks, and the kids ran back on them. The train refused to stop, and just missed killing people three times. To us, it symbolized the war machine, which also refused to stop, killing people along the way.

Photographers and TV cameras were there, recording the scene and exaggerating the violence by concentrating on it. Photographs of protesters blocking the trains went across the country, turning on young kids in every city. Soldiers hung a sign out the window which read: "We Don't Want to Go!," which was broadcast within hours to the entire nation. That's communication!

We saw Berkeley as a media symbol for the country. Despite its tiny size, what happened in Berkeley was heard in Washington and on campuses across the world. We sat in Chinese restaurants and coffee shops and knew that we had power to set off waves of thought across the country.

If someone had been making a Hollywood movie, he would not have been able to script the drama of the antiwar movement so theatrically. We outacted the American government for the eight years that we dominated center stage. We sent the announcement to kids all over America: join the revolution and have fun. Marches, rallies, police confrontations, major headlines all attracted people. Once they got attracted by the action, they discovered the issues.

We rented a six-room house near the Berkeley campus. The place became a legend, growing by rumor. Soon teen-agers ran away from home, high school kids quit school, and college students dropped out to join us making history.

On October 15, 1965, people marched from the Berkeley campus to shut down the Oakland Army Terminal and stop war materiel from being shipped to Vietnam; we were prepared to go to jail en masse. Instead, a phalanx of Oakland cops met us at the city limits with gas and police dogs. We turned back. On the march we heard that demonstrations were taking place at the same time in thirty other cities. The antiwar movement was becoming a national phenomenon, mobilizing public opinion, and forcing politicians to take a stand.

From 1965 to 1970, I lived activist politics twenty-four hours a day. I became a full-time agitator, quitting graduate school to work exclusively for the movement. When I was eating, I was talking politics; when I was sleeping, I was dreaming politics; when I was walking down the street, I was thinking politics. I was a single-

77

minded, one-dimensional fanatic dedicated to figuring out actions that would make life unbearable for the President of the United States.

Because of the Berkeley actions, which right-wing Congressmen publicized by calling them treasonous, I was subpoenaed as a witness to a hearing of the House Committee on Un-American Activities in August, 1966. This included a free trip to Washington and a hotel room paid for by the government. Our public line was that it was an outrageous attack on our civil liberties; but unofficially, we coined the phrase: "subpoenas envy." I wanted to do something before the committee that would grab the antiwar attention of the country. I decided to wear the uniform of an American Revolutionary soldier to the hearings, renting the costume at a theatrical costume store in Berkeley for $35.

When I showed up in the costume, the marshalls at first would not let me into the hearing room even though I was under subpoena. When I got in I handed out copies of the Declaration of Independence to members of the committee, reporters, spectators, and the federal marshalls.

The press ate it up: it was on page one across the country. With that one zap I inspired rebellious people everywhere to be outrageous. I had used the media to spread my message.

Three days later, the committee cancelled its hearings without calling me to testify, and I stood up and objected. Stone-faced federal marshalls were forced to carry Thomas Paine out of the hearing room, and arrested him (me) while he was screaming "I want to testify! I want to testify!"

In the mid-sixties, antiwar student activity was joined by the emergence of hippies, wearing colorful clothes, dropping out of school, getting high on grass and acid, communicating with God, and creating a new life-style. Berkeley radicals saw them as a diversion from politics; hippies saw the radicals as uptight politicians. I saw the hippies as a true political expression of the breakdown of the affluent society. But I also thought the radicals were right in focusing their attention on power and foreign policy. I therefore vowed to work to fuse the two forces.

At that time I was twenty-eight years old and just beginning to smoke grass. It was my first venture into hedonism. Until then I was a driven man: I had fun, but life was work. When I finally got stoned I smiled to myself and thought: Oh, so this is what life is all about! My consciousness expanded, and I was able to get close to people in intimate situations. With grass I thought we had discovered a revolutionary herb. I became an instant pothead, and advocated that everyone else do the same.

I decided, on a whim, to run for mayor of Berkeley in 1966, when I noticed three days before the election that no one from the movement, except an irrelevant Trotskyist, was running against the incumbent, a bald-headed conservative factory owner. By entering the race, I hoped to demean the office. I said I'd resign if elected. I ran a "serious campaign," however, with a pro-marijuana and antiwar platform. We had door-to-door precinct workers and by election day I thought I had a chance to win. I finished second, out of four, with 22 per cent of the vote, winning four student precincts.

When I took acid for the first time, after the Summer of Love in 1967, I experienced the make-believe quality of all reality and became a consciousness explorer. As a representative of the Berkeley radicals, I spoke at the first be-in in Golden Gate Park with Allen Ginsberg and Timothy Leary and got a cool reception from the stoned-out hippies. I was a hippie activist, creating a new life-style while challenging the power structure of society. What a romantic, exciting time to be alive!

Around that time I got my first education in jail. After a demonstration in which we drove General Maxwell Taylor out of San Francisco by spilling cow's blood on his limousine, I served thirty days in the San Francisco County jail. Those first few hours locked up behind a steel door with only the Bible to read drove me batty. But gradually I adjusted. Around me in jail were blacks with deep grudges against American society. My determination to humanize America increased. I decided to leave Berkeley and go to New York, and eventually to take the Berkeley direct action spirit to the Pentagon, the heart of the war machine.

The day I arrived in New York a friend told me, "Abbie Hoffman thinks it's more important to burn dollar bills than draft cards." Abbie at the time was planning an assault on the New York Stock Exchange. We gathered in Wall Street, Abbie stuffed dollar bills in our hands, and we took the tour guide trip, followed by press and cameras, to the top of the exchange. There we threw dollar bills over the ledge, watching as the brokers below ran after the dollar bills. It might have been for only half-a-second, but we had stopped the market!

Police grabbed the ten of us, dragged us down the stairs, and deposited us on Wall Street at high noon in front of astonished businessmen and hungry TV cameras. That night the attack by hippies on the Stock Exchange was told around the world—international publicity! The next week the New York Stock Exchange announced they were building a bullet-proof window above the tourist section as a protection against future invasions. I fell in love with Abbie.

The peace movement action for October 21, 1967, was planned as a nonviolent assault on the Pentagon. Our mission was to surround the five-cornered building and exorcise the spirits within. One hundred thousand middle-class folk marched from the Capitol across the Potomac bridges. Once across the bridges, peace squads broke out to "attack" the Pentagon on all five sides.

We spoke to the army through our microphones and bullhorns, trying to motivate the soldiers to desert and join us. Five hours before Pentagon employees returned to work, the army arrested us quietly one by one: the arrest total was 832. I was sentenced to thirty days in jail. Secretary of Defense Robert McNamara watched the entire battle from his fifth-floor window, accompanied by one of his younger assistants, Daniel Ellsberg.

The next act in growing antiwar consciousness would be to steal the media in Chicago during the week of the 1968 Democratic Convention. We sent the call out to kids all over the country to come to Chicago for a party. It would be our Festival of Life against the Convention of Death.

To carry this out we needed a new organization. The stuffy political organizations were too cumbersome to make decisions, too straight to understand media theater. On New Year's Eve, 1967, seven of us got together in Abbie's apartment on St. Marks Place. We studied the problem in a stoned way. It was a youth revolution, an international revolution, and we wanted to have a party. That became Y.I.P., Youth International Party, and Paul Krassner shouted "Yippie!" and we ran around the room dancing. We had it!

A myth is an idea that exists in people's heads. As long as the myth exists, it makes no difference whether or not the physical reality exists. If people act on the myth, they will create the reality. The media creates myths; then the reality catches up to the myth and gives it flesh. Yippie was a myth created in our heads that became reality.

Yet "yippies" sounds so frivolous—would people actually call themselves "yippies"? Can you imagine the President warning the country about the danger from the "yippies"? Nobody would take him seriously, and the whole country would be reduced to one big joke. Ed Sanders added the slogan, "Abandon the creeping meatball!" and we were on the bandwagon—yippies were coming to Chicago.

When Chicago came, only five thousand people showed up. LBJ had already been forced out of the Presidency by antiwar pressure. Bobby Kennedy was dead. No major rock groups came to Chicago. And Abbie and I were not speaking to each other; we had separated off into yippie factions. We were a conspiracy, but by the time of the action the conspirators no longer talked to each other! The Chicago police went berserk in the streets, turning newsmen into yippies with their billy clubs. I was kidnapped off the streets by five cops on the last night. My bodyguard for the week, a biker named Bob, turned out to be a Chicago policeman, and his testimony eventually sent me to jail for two months.

One cost of the Vietnam War was blood in the streets and the estrangement of youth from our political system. The Democratic Party never recovered from Chicago, and Nixon was elected. Six months after taking office, he approved the indictment of eight radicals for conspiring to riot in Chicago. I thanked him for the honor, calling it "The Academy Award of Protest."

I am speaking now only for myself, writing what I could never write during the trial or while our appeals were being considered.

During the five-and-a-half month trial I agreed more with the government's analysis of our behavior than with our defense. The government held us responsible for what happened in Chicago. Our defense saw us primarily as victims.

The government said: these men are radicals who wanted a disturbance in Chicago to disrupt American society and protest the war. Our defense was that we were citizens whose civil liberties were violated by the government's police riot against us. The government was right in theory, but wrong in specifics. Despite the most exhaustive FBI hunt for information since the Kennedy assassination, they had all the facts wrong. Throughout my activist life I was always amazed by the FBI's stupidity. They never knew what was going on.

The most electric person at our trial turned out to be the judge, a five-foot-tall, crotchety, eighty-year-old man with a Shakespearean flourish, a searing wit, and a quick temper. Julius Hoffman insulted and scorned us, and lectured us piously from the bench. He gagged and chained Bobby Seale, Black Panther chairman, to his seat to stop Bobby from demanding the right to be his own attorney. Hoffman became a national media symbol of intolerance, and did more to destroy faith in the American court system than we ever could have. To help Julie blow the trial, we did things like wear judicial robes to court and laugh at him when he wasn't looking, prompting Julius to say, "Marshall, find out who is laughing, and make them stop laughing!"

The trial's many personalities kept the media interested, and it became a national political drama on the nightly news. In the end three jurors wanted to free us and nine wanted to convict us, so they compromised and found us innocent of conspiracy and guilty of crossing state lines with the intention to riot.

Two years later the Appeals Court disqualified the entire trial and scolded Hoffman. A new trial for contempt resulted in guilty sentences, but not jail terms, for Abbie, Dave Dellinger, attorney William Kunstler, and myself. Everyone gained from the trial. The judge became a hero to the right wing, and was invited to dinner with Nixon at the White House. The prosecution chilled civil libertarians throughout the country with fear. The radical side inspired youth with our example of defiance.

The trial was the highlight of my life. Every day was another adventure, another chapter of comic theater underlying the national drama. All across the country people felt sorry for me, felt my freedom was in danger and that I was a victim of government repression. My eyes did often have a hard, cold, frightened stare and I was paranoid much of the time. I believed I might end up spending ten years in jail. But I was willing to serve jail time in exchange for the excitement of making history and the feeling that we were standing up against immorality and oppression. When I finally did serve sixty-six days in jail in the summer of 1966, I stayed high by thinking of the Vietnamese fighting and dying for their country; this was the least I could do for them.

I ask myself how I became an armchair guerrilla. I say "armchair" because I never shot a gun or planted a bomb, but I supported the Vietcong and selective violence here at home. Though I am a white middle-class American, who enjoys a good meal and the luxury of comfort, I nevertheless share the feelings of extremist revolutionaries.

My country had brutalized the red race and the black race and now we were dropping bombs on brown and yellow people. I felt my position was morally right. Anything any of us could do to stop genocide was O.K. As a child of America I had been taught that the "Good Germans" who did nothing to stop Hitler were also morally responsible for his crimes. I felt anger at the gap between our ideals and the cold reality of our power system.

After the Chicago demonstrations of 1968, I was becoming a leader of the movement but I was afraid to give a speech. My insides trembled at the thought of standing in front of people and rapping. What if I opened my mouth and nothing came out? Wouldn't people laugh at me? I even read Dale Carnegie's book on public speaking.

I got invited to Vancouver to give three speeches, and there I experienced a breakthrough. I began by telling myself how important the things I had to say were and that it made no difference what happened. "Breathe, Jerry, breathe. Look at your audience: take your time, become one with them." A speaker can manipulate an audience like a conductor manipulates a symphony orchestra. To get confidence I picked out one person who laughed at all my jokes and gave the entire speech to him or her. Mentions of marijuana always united the crowd. I spoke from my gut, saying what students knew but were afraid to say.

Then I discovered a new crisis. Just when I was ready to deliver the climax, I could go in one of two directions: increase the passion to bring the audience to a peak or back off. As I reached that point of power, I often felt myself hold back.

And then I discovered Ritalin, a little white pill. I lost my self-consciousness and merged with my speech, and when the climactic moments came, I went over the edge. I took Ritalin a lot during those wild days of 1968 and 1969, traveling the college campuses, writing *Do It!*, and cooking up antigovernment schemes. It made me feel that I could do anything. I was a speed freak in a speedy era. I roared around the country, occasionally stopping to observe with some irony that I was probably on the same drug as the politicians, businessmen, and militarists I was attacking.

But slowly I began to realize what I was losing by taking a pill. Ritalin was distorting my relationship with Ruthie. Ritalin was pushing me over my emotional center, resulting in a superenthusiastic, overenergetic personality. Ritalin was reshaping my personality, so I stopped taking it.

I think that every public official should make not only a complete financial disclosure, but also a full disclosure of all pills and drugs he or she takes. Drugs mold the personality. What pills do our public officials take before speeches, and what effect does that have on their ego?

From the end of the trial to the summer of 1970, I traveled from campus to campus. After speeches kids would come up and thank me for changing their lives.

At the same time *Do It!* appeared, promoting anarchy and selling 200,000 copies. I went on TV in almost every city of the country. I didn't know if I was headed for Hollywood or jail.

After some of my speeches on campus, the students would close down the school with a strike, or blow up the ROTC building, or riot. Meanwhile, I was being paid $500 to $1,000 from the official student organization for giving the speech. This was for me the greatest contradiction in my life: getting money for showing up at campus to tell students to burn down their school.

What a crazy country! I am paid $500 for appearing for an hour and a half and getting students to laugh at my jokes and give me a standing ovation. My father drove a bread truck for weeks to earn $500.

After every speech kids came up to me asking, "What should *I* do?" They looked to me and other "leaders" to provide leadership. I choked when I heard the question; I couldn't tell them what to do. I had no idea what to do myself.

Many radicals criticized me in the late 1960's for becoming a media superstar, traveling the country to give speeches, but not helping build an organization to carry out my politics. I accept that criticism. I saw myself as a propagandist, a national myth-maker, turning people on to their power. My value was to draw new people into the movement. I could not do that and build an organization too, so I looked to others to build it.

Radical life was getting complicated for me. Because of my activities, I was recognized easily at demonstrations. Other activists often stared at me, and people came up for autographs. I attracted cameras and undercover cops like flies. Police saw me and blew their whistles. Young kids waited for me to lead them in riot. No longer anonymous, I was no longer free; I was now living my life in a fishbowl. Everyone had expectations of me. I started to feel more like an "important leader" and less like another street freak. Fame, in a sense, destroyed my effectiveness.

In the spring of 1970 the movement climaxed. In response to the American military invasion of Cambodia, one hundred campuses exploded in demonstrations against the war. Overnight, campuses turned into battlegrounds between students and police as ROTC buildings went up in smoke. Speaking on a campus, I felt the energy in the room waiting for the fuse to ignite energy into action.

At the same time the government was attempting to destroy the Black Panther Party. With Bobby Seale on trial, the members of the Chicago Seven helped organize a rally in New Haven of fifty thousand people. The next week half a million people marched on Washington to protest Cambodia. Opposition to the war was breaking out in the middle class. The movement was no longer a hippie student phenomenon. Businessmen, workers, and women began protesting in their own way.

The antiwar moratoriums brought pressure on Congress. Nixon changed his Vietnam policy to withdraw American soldiers from Vietnam and stop bombing. He proposed his China trip to steal the thunder from the left.

In the spring of 1970 antiwar activists were the most powerful energy source in the country. During the years 1969 and 1970 the Nixon government used tactics like enemy lists, illegal break-ins, phone taps, violent attacks in demonstrations by FBI agents and policemen, CIA surveillance, Internal Revenue harassment, and vigilantism to smash the political movement. By June, 1970, thousands of young people had made a decision to back away from further confrontation with the government. As Nixon was implementing a plan to destroy the political movement, the Houston Plan, the movement itself pulled a disappearing act, choosing to disperse rather than face possible extinction.

At Kent State the American cowboys settled it with guns. In bright daylight and before TV cameras they murdered four white students. Their guns spoke a violent lesson: demonstrate and you too may die. Even though huge rallies took place all across the country in protest of Kent State, bullets spoke louder than words. The movement was doomed after Kent State.

Women abandoned the male-dominated New Left movement, leaving men without a work force. We were as chauvinistic as the society itself, radicals as far as Vietnam and blacks were concerned, but imitation John Waynes in our personal lives. Without women, the movement was over. Although they were dominated by men and the male image, women were the soul and heart of the movement, and often its fist, brain, and voice.

Friction and infighting within the ranks rose to colossal proportions; everyone was bad-mouthing everyone else. We scared ourselves, and our "Are you ready to die or kill?" attitude drove the liberal students away. The internal movement stance was: if you're not into violence, you're not doing anything. The more outrageous we were, the more outrageous we had to be to continue to be outrageous. Manipulators of the media, we ended up getting manipulated.

Jerry Rubin

When I said "riot" on college campuses in 1969 and the students rioted, I started thinking, "Wait, this is serious—it's no longer a game when university buildings are blown up, and police begin arresting students on felonies, and towns are split into armed camps." By 1970 there was tremendous pressure on all activists to translate their radical talk into action—shoot a gun or plant a bomb. Two of my closest friends were arrested trying to fire-bomb a bank and were sentenced to jail. Other people in the movement condemned their action as suicidal. The feeling in those days was that our rhetoric was driving us to actions from which there was no return.

Most of us were not ready for an armed confrontation with the state. I felt that I was being set up for martyrdom by death or jail. I briefly considered going underground and becoming a fugitive, but I decided that I was not ready to make that commitment.

I was scared. By 1969 the FBI had infiltrated every political group in the country. Paranoia was rife, as phones were tapped and mail opened. Police infiltrated demonstrations; a new recruit to the movement had to go through a thousand security checks and even then we couldn't be sure.

Mass enthusiasm disappeared almost overnight. Creativity fell off in all areas of life—from music to art to writing. The Beatles broke up. Hippie communities like Haight-Ashbury became ghost towns. Those who said "burn down the school" one year enrolled as students the next. The psychological depression of 1970 to 1973 preceded the economic depression of 1975.

The economic pinch drove protesters back into the system to survive. Beards came off, and people went back into their fathers' businesses. The next generation saw us as a New Establishment and rebelled against us by going Establishment. The mass movement as we had known it was over. Action brought reaction. People wanted to look at the reactions. To be, to think, to meditate, to feel became greater desires than to do. My role as a "do it" catalyst was over for the time being.

The movement ended when its particular historical task was over. We curtailed U.S. involvement in Vietnam and created the atmosphere that led to the Watergate revelations and the fall of Nixon. Some people feel that because the movement ended, it failed. That is not true. The 1960's transformed America's consciousness in immeasurable ways. Then we discovered that although we had exposed the hypocrisy and inequality of American society, we ourselves had been conditioned by that society, and we had to release ourselves from that conditioning. This led to the Inner Revolution of the 1970's.

For most of the 1960's I was treated as a criminal by the state; my telephone was bugged, I was followed by the FBI, and I was jailed. But I knew that the state was the true criminal. When we were active, those at the helm of the government were Richard Nixon, Spiro Agnew, Bob Haldeman, John Ehrlichman, John Mitchell, J. Edgar Hoover, and Richard Kliendienst. If we had predicted in 1968 that Nixon and Agnew would be forced to resign, and that Mitchell, Haldeman, Ehrlichman, and Kleindienst would be convicted of crimes in court, people would have said that LSD had twisted our minds and turned our reality into fantasy. But fantasy is no match for reality.

Chapter 8

Fame and Money

I̵N the sixties, singers sang protest songs and revolutionaries made revolution. Then protest singers and revolutionaries got rewarded with media attention and money, and they began singing not about inequality but about overattention. I feel the same way myself.

I have been famous in each phase of my life: in my high school as a reporter, in Cincinnati as a reporter, in Berkeley as radical agitator, and nationally as radical, author, and symbol. Being famous is my karma, my personality, my defense against a hostile world. I live my life in public. It covers up my fear, gives me an outlet for my energy, and provides me with a base of power which I need to survive. What is fame?

As a kid I worshipped baseball players and vowed someday to be as famous as they were. It's great to see people's eyes light up when they see you; to be recognized by people you do not know; to hear a buzz when you walk into a restaurant and people realize who you are.

Fame is an asset. I can call up practically anyone on the phone and get through. People respect famous people—they are automatically interested in what I have to say. Nobody knows exactly what I have done, but they know I'm *famous*.

In his heart every famous person is a groupie. I became famous so that I could meet other famous people on an equal basis. They're meeting "Jerry Rubin," and I'm meeting "Walter Cronkite." Very often with famous people the fame-mask drops and people get to know each other quickly. There is an immediate intimacy; you feel you can say or ask anything. I love meeting other famous people!

And I love to play with the media; it is a big toy and I am a media freak. It isn't even necessary to create events to transform consciousness; in fact, an event doesn't exist until the media announces it. Once the media announces it, it is an event whether or not it exists.

A few months before the national political conventions in 1972, I arrived in Miami Beach and called a press conference in front of Convention Hall. The media had already outlined its drama: will Miami 1972 be another Chicago 1968? As someone convicted for instigating riots in Chicago, I was in a perfect position to use the paranoia of the politicians and the theatrics of the media to have some electronic fun.

I took off my shirt and announced that ten thousand yippies were going to parade nude during the convention. The specter of police clubbing naked bodies danced through the heads of reporters. No one doubted my ability to pull off the event. That night the three TV stations headlined their local news with warnings of a nude march. A non-event! Immediately, people were writing letters to the newspaper attacking the nude march.

I doubt that I could have found five hundred yippies to parade nude. But TV reporters are interested in drama. The public needs the image of nude yippies to act out their own repressed fantasies; at the same time, it allows them to play the role of moralists.

I purposefully manipulated the media, but on a deeper level I see that it was mutual manipulation. To interest the media I needed to express my politics frivolously. I became an image of a liberated body in spite of my own body shyness. Without being aware of it, I gave the media what they wanted. If I had given a sober lecture on the history of Vietnam, the media cameras would have turned off.

The media gives the people what it thinks people want, so you have a chain of people caught in their expectations of what they think their audience wants. As a revolutionary, I reinforced that chain by using it for my political ends. I don't know how to break the media chain. Of course, one way is not to play, but if you do play, it's hard to succeed while breaking the roles or rules.

So many times during an interview I subconsciously gave the reporter what I thought he wanted. I played into the hands of the theatrical media who compete against each other to dramatize their stories. While pleasing the media, I consciously created my image of total permission. In a repressed society, I wanted to stand out as a symbol of freedom. My mythical existence enabled people to redefine the possibilities for their lives.

I became a symbol for kids leaving home, students dropping out of school, people quitting jobs. As a symbol, I became a source of personal power for young people and a hostility trigger for older people.

I did what was necessary to jab people's thought processes by provoking their emotions. I never felt that communication with people was exclusively a rational process. I wanted to involve them emotionally—hence outrageous theater, yippie, and a scandalous image. We saw the narrow alternatives in America, the emphasis on conformity and death, and our goal was to shock people into change.

The image of a crazy, violent, face-painted, screaming, angry, fierce, funny revolutionary street-fighting fucking freak, a theatrical amalgam of Lenny Bruce and Che Guevara, was created in concert by me and the media. I manipulated the media and the media manipulated me. I used the dramatics of the media to dramatize myself, and the media got what it wanted to make a good story.

But by creating events that made news, I fell into the media's trap. Since reporters can only interpret from their own level of awareness, they saw us as "leaders" and "followers." In every situation the press led with the question, "Who's the leader?" The mass movement of the 1960's functioned from the bottom up. Leaders did plan, dramatize, and organize, but there were *thousands* of leaders. Yet the American media, with its dependence on personality and celebrities, heaped it all on specific individuals perpetuating the notion of a manipulated mass.

We radicals had figured out that we couldn't compete economically, militarily, or politically with the power of the war-makers. So we invented our own source of power: communication. We learned to use the media to create an audience for our message. One demonstrator could steal the national media any day with a bold act.

Fame was both a cover-up for my fear and a protection against police harassment. As a public symbol, I felt I was less likely to be anonymously jailed, beaten, or arrested. Within the protective structure of public attention I used my fame as boldly as I could, as a springboard for courage. A negative effect of that tactic was that my public image led young kids into brash actions which were not protected by fame or power.

Fame is a two-edged sword. I lived in danger of being made a public martyr by the government. I served nine months in jail for being "Jerry Rubin." I saw my close partner-in-excitement, Abbie Hoffman, forced underground because he was Abbie Hoffman. Fame can backfire.

My image worked until it grew beyond my control. The media then decided to create an image of the revolutionary who becomes rich, grows old, joins the Establishment.

News in America consists of creating and destroying

myths. The media creates the drama and then finds people to play the roles. If I had not filled the role of enfant terrible in the sixties, someone else would have. In 1970 the media announced to the world that the movement was dead. Reporters asked activists, "Why did it die?" I read about myself in the newspapers as an "aging ex-radical."

It's confusing to have a double identity—me and my image. I understand the process because I too see people in images. I get hooked on the media image of certain "celebrities," living out my own personal fantasies through them. Even though I do it to others, I resent people who resent me just because I'm famous. It's scary to know that thousands of people hate me just for being known.

I recoil inside when people relate to me as a famous person even though I created it. I want to be seen as I am. I get nervous when I have to play the role of celebrity. I don't like it when I am relaxing and people want me to perform the role of "Jerry Rubin." When you become famous, you give up your freedom. You belong to other people. Or, at least, they act as if they own you.

For instance, I am in a restaurant talking intimately with a friend and someone recognizes me and comes up to ask my opinion on the trial, therapy, or the world economic crisis. They think that because I am famous they can interrupt any discussion to talk to me. If I am polite, my personal conversation with my friend is over and I am in a new discussion with a stranger. It's hard to tell people that you do not have time for them.

And then there's the reverse situation. Often, when people do not recognize me, I feel funny. So, early in the conversation I say who I am. People's interest in me expands geometrically when they hear my name. So my fame becomes a crutch. Sometimes, though, I'm embarrassed to tell them. It feels like name-dropping.

Sometimes people act distant and withdraw from me, because they think, "If I show an interest, he'll think it's only because he's Jerry Rubin." So they ignore me, and I feel: "That person does not like me." Many people find it hard to be natural with me. They either show an overwhelming interest or ignore me. I push their "He's-too-famous-for-me" buttons and they push my "I'm-no-good" button; in the process a potential human relationship is lost.

A famous person often must be willing to trade his private life for the maintenance and care of his public image. You spend endless hours worrying about your image. It starts to have an independent life with very little relation to you. You discover that every person has his own version of you. If you are not very careful, eventually even you forget who you are.

The problem of fame is that you get frozen in one frame and nothing you do can alter the name. Many Americans see me as an anti-American bomb-thrower who shouts all the time and never takes baths. I am nothing of the sort. But that image serves a purpose deeper than truth. People need me to fulfill the image of devil so they can play the anti-devil. I am the devil they fear they really are.

If I wanted to track down and uproot the lies that are written about me, I would have no time to do anything else. The moment you become a public figure you give up your freedom. If you are sensitive about your image in print—reach for the Valium!

In March, 1974, Dick Cavett did a special hour-and-a-half program with Rennie Davis, Tom Hayden, Abbie Hoffman, and myself. Even though we said nothing more radical than many congressmen say every day, because of *our images* the ABC management flipped out and tried to cancel the show. Finally they censored two lines, one saying that Rockefeller owns a good deal of America, and then added a half-hour interview with two conservatives, who attacked us as traitors.

Since I was a creator of absurd theater, people think it is quite yippie to yippie me. In the summer of 1974, I spoke at a press conference with Allen Ginsberg, Jack Leary, Ken Kelley, and Ram Dass. I was attacking the government and Tim Leary, who allegedly had informed on his friends while behind bars. In the middle of my statement a kangaroo emerged out of the press corps and began hopping toward me.

I kept speaking, ignoring the kangaroo, until he was in front of me making motions to throw a cream pie in my face. Ken Kelley leaped up and pushed the kangaroo away. At that moment the kangaroo's mask fell off and underneath was a friend of mine, Dr. Hippocrates, Gene Schoenfeld.

Later that day my doorbell rang. I looked through the peephole. It was Dr. Hip in his kangaroo head, come to watch himself on the evening news on my color TV. I let him in for a moment to chew him out and then threw him out, really confusing him. Besides thinking the press conference was a "kangaroo court," he thought that since I was a yippie, I would appreciate his theatrical act of trying to steal the media spotlight. But I felt Gene did the stunt mainly to promote his just-released book.

Jerry Rubin

Underneath my court jester's façade in the sixties I was a serious activist, using clowning to make my point. I cultivated a wild man of Borneo look to scare parents and inspire kids to drop out. Years later, when I began to see the hippie Che style on TV commercials, I knew that it was over; longhair symbols were no longer effective.

My long hair had been as much a costume for me as suits and short hair are for the middle class. If I was attached to my hair, I was a prisoner of my self-image. I went into the bathroom and shaved my beard. I looked at my lips for the first time in years. I liked what I saw. I went to a hair stylist and got a haircut. I entered rooms and no one knew who I was, because I didn't fit their image of me. I was thirty-five but I looked twenty-three. Even when I told people I was Jerry Rubin, they refused to believe me. "Not THE Jerry Rubin?" they'd say. I thought about changing my first name to THE.

I still needed an external symbol to show people I was different. So I pierced my left ear and wore an Indian turquoise earring. I even fantasized thousands of men wearing earrings as the next revolutionary symbol. The earring revolution! But I finally took the earring off. Now I enjoy being unpredictable, independent of my physical appearance. When I get attached to my clean-shaven look, I'll go back to my Berkeley anarchist handlebar moustache—or become the Borneo wild man again.

Fame is addictive. It is my heroin, my main line. I need attention from the outside, a platform, recognition as an outlet for my energy. I made myself famous because I believed that people needed a reason to notice me. I was trying to get from the outside what I felt I lacked on the inside.

I no longer get a kick out of seeing my name in the paper. I prefer the warmth of personal relationships to public gossip. Although I love to be in the vanguard, I don't want to be saddled forever with the "radical of the sixties" image.

Fame has become a source of power in America, a new class, elected by the media. Famous people are a new elite, with similar problems, life-styles, and attitudes.

Famous people are dangerous. The more famous, the more dangerous, because they have consciousness power. As a famous person I am part of a privileged class. A truly democratic society is without rich or famous people: all are rich, all are famous.

I'd like to share my fame with other people as long as I've got it, and also use it for positive purposes. Someone asked me not too long ago what I do for a living. I thought about it for a moment, then replied: "I'm famous. That's my job."

Money has been the most crazed area of my life, with power and sex running a close second and third. In this respect, I am a typical American.

A lot of my energy goes into making or keeping money. Money for me is survival. Anything that threatens me in the money department seems to threaten my survival.

My childhood conditions left me tight and insecure about money. I cringe when I have to discuss money matters with friends. Behind every dispute I've had in my life, I can find a dispute over the dollar.

Jerry Rubin

I have not created a comfortable consumer environment for myself because I have a hard time enjoying money. I used to justify that programming with revolutionary politics: it is more noble to be poor and struggling. To enjoy the comforts of life is to be "bourgeois" or "counterrevolutionary." Lurking behind my revolutionary image, however, is my puritan upbringing.

I've always been able to get paid for what I like to do. For five years I worked as a reporter, but I loved my work so much I'd have done it for free. The paychecks were icing on the cake. During the movement I supported myself as an organizer, writer, and lecturer, with a similar love.

For the past year and a half I have lived in a simple two-room apartment in North Beach. I own a color TV, stereo, typewriter, water bed, and little other furniture. I own my own car, and eat most of my meals in restaurants. My main expense is money spent for education and consciousness. I need money so I can be politically and spiritually active. Money for me is freedom.

Many Americans, caught up in credit buying and overconsumption, spend most of their lives working in order to support and buy many things they don't really need. I have deliberately designed my life to be free of this. That's one reason I don't amass a lot of electronic and consumer junk that demands upkeep. The nature of American economic society is to trap people through advertising into buying habits that force them to spend all their time scurrying for money.

I don't want to get trapped in that circle, although in many ways I can't avoid it. I've thrown money away in foolish investments because the demon in me wanted to sabotage my success to please my internalized parents. In the process of doing psychic therapy and est I challenged this puritan conditioning, and told myself, it's O.K. to enjoy the rewards of life that money brings.

The death of my parents eventually brought insurance policy money to my brother and me. I used money from the insurance policy to support myself while organizing demonstrations against the inequalities of the capitalist system. The money, $20,000 for each of us, was held in trust by a lawyer in Cincinnati, a conservative Republican who deplored what I was doing but protected the money in stocks as I went around the country attacking the stock market. I could not have legally stopped him. As sole guardian of the trust, he could have sold us out. I appreciated his protecting our money. Had the media discovered the fact that I owned stocks (where were you, CIA?), I could have been badly hurt in the press in 1968.

My secret stocks didn't affect my anger against capitalism, but they were an internal karmic irony. Who says human beings are without contradictions?

In 1973 the stock market suffered a heart attack and a fifth of my money was wiped out.

When I got the advance for my book *Do It!*, I wanted to use the money to oppose the system. I went to a tax lawyer and we set up a nonprofit corporation to protect the money. The foundation was approved by the Internal Revenue Service. I donated my book to the foundation, which then put me on a salary. I paid other radical friends salaries to support them in their political work.

I find it strange that people find it strange that revolutionaries try to use the same loopholes that the capitalists use to avoid taxes. In an illegal and corrupt system, are radicals supposed to be the only honest people, paying taxes to support the military budget to kill Asians? I decided to set up a nonprofit tax-exempt corporation called the Social Education Foundation.

The Young Americans for Freedom discovered my legal tax dodge and passed the information to a Southern Congressman who protested to the Internal Revenue Service, which promptly began an investigation. Within three months the IRS removed my foundation's tax-exempt status.

Then the story hit the media and I was revealed publicly as the "radical with the tax dodge." It made perfect sense for me to do it, yet it sounded like hypocrisy. Radicals are no longer radicals if they succeed economically; therefore, to be a radical one must fail. By that definition the status quo has the situation perfectly defined. The power to define the situation is the ultimate power.

I folded the foundation and realized that the tax laws work one way for the rich and another way for protestors. Privately, an official of the IRS told my lawyer that my foundation was legal, but the political pressure on the IRS was too great to let Jerry Rubin have a tax-exempt foundation. But there was nothing I could do about it. Who was going to have sympathy for Jerry Rubin's money problems? Eight years later, after Watergate, the country as a whole learned how thoroughly the IRS was used as a political weapon by right-wing government forces.

"Money doesn't talk, it swears," says Dylan. As a result of my notoriety from the Chicago conspiracy trial I began to get money for making speeches and writing. While I stayed true to my commitment, I did feel the edge come off my anger against the system. It was not a conscious process, but slowly, insidiously, the presence of money in my pockets made me feel privileged and mellowed out my radicalism.

The mere existence of excess money in my pockets —independent of my thoughts—transformed my feelings. I had new problems: money problems. I felt separated from poorer friends. I felt guilty eating in a fancy restaurant. I was no longer a "street person." I became a "have." Not that I was rich, but I was no longer poor. I now had a tax lawyer, a business adviser, a publisher, a regular attorney—I was beginning to build an institution around myself.

I had something to lose—and thereby lost a certain freedom.

One of my biggest problems was what to do with the money. If you don't invest, inflation eats away your money; if you do, you're playing the capitalist game. I invested, hoping to win big so I wouldn't have to play the game and could have money to spread around to friends and political projects.

Catch 22: One needs money to spread ideas against the money system. In the capitalist jungle there is very little one can do without money. Every time I invested I lost. Did I learn a lesson about how greed destroys!

I met a dope dealer, who came highly recommended. I wanted to trust him, so I trusted him. We talked five or six times, laying out an investment plan, and he seemed reliable and dependable, a "nice guy." Anyone else would not have trusted him for a minute, but I was so lost in my financial fantasies that I saw only what I wanted to see: the $100,000 I might get in

Jerry Rubin

three months, enough to take care of all my needs with a lot left over for the movement.

I went to the bank and took out $8,000 in eighty one-hundred dollar bills. I put the money in an envelope, walked across the street to a coffee shop, and slipped him the money. We kissed on the lips and he left.

The rest of the day my teeth ground painfully into each other and my stomach churned furiously. Despite the fantasies of the head, the body doesn't lie.

I never saw him again.

I lost another $5,000 investing in a friend of mine who wanted to produce pornographic sheets. Then I lost a few thousand more in an art portfolio. In the end, I lost almost all the money I invested; I am a piss-poor businessman.

> All money represents theft. To steal from the rich is a sacred and religious act. To take what you need is an act of self-love, self-liberation. While looting, a man to his own self is true.
>
> JERRY RUBIN, *Do It!*

In the summer of 1973 the home I temporarily lived in was broken into and my woman friend's clothes, stereo, jewelry, and furniture were stolen. A few months later I learned that an ex-movement acquaintance of mine had done the robbery! I rushed over to her house and found the jewelry ruined, the clothes torn, most of the personal belongings destroyed. I confronted the thief and she had no excuse. The robbery, she said, was a lark; she wanted to see if she could get away with it. She had been in high school while

I was running around the country advocating anarchy. In advocating stealing as a revolutionary act, I guess I didn't make clear the difference between stealing from General Motors and stealing from me.

> Kids should steal money from their parents, because that is liberation from the money ethic: true family.
>
> —JERRY RUBIN, *Do It!*

The comedy of the situation tickled me when I wasn't angry. It's always humorous when your karma comes home.

Abbie wrote a book called *Steal This Book*. Many people congratulate me on the book, but I had nothing to do with it. What irony when two people who helped Abbie edit the book later publicly accused Abbie of stealing the book from them. In his many moments of laughing at himself, Abbie says, "I stole *Steal This Book*?! That sounds like something I would think up!"

During the movement I turned thousands of dollars into green energy. I gave the $20,000 advance on my second book, *We Are Everywhere*, to build an organization around yippie. I spent tons of money for lawyers in my various court trials. I helped pay for the expenses of people who traveled to Algeria to set up Timothy Leary's prison escape from the U.S. in order to join Eldridge Cleaver in Algeria. I spent the remains of my parents' insurance money supporting myself during my therapy-consciousness trips. By 1975, I was broke again.

I do not know if it is possible to transform my personal attitudes toward money without changing the

107

capitalist system. I worry. What if I change and no one else does? What if I share and everyone else doesn't? I'll be the "nice guy" that loses.

For me, money means freedom from economic necessity so that I can grow, develop, experience. In a capitalist society my freedom depends on the economic slavery of others. A competitive system means some win and some lose. My goal is a society in which the necessities and luxuries of life are available to all, a society based on cooperation rather than competition, love rather than fear. I don't know if such a society is inconsistent with "human nature" because I have never seen "human nature" independent of a social structure.

I do know that having money tends to make you forget those people without money. Yet, to change the system we need money to survive and create energy. I am going to have to live with my contradictions of needing money to survive under capitalism while at the same time trying to subvert that system by substituting non-money, pro-human values.

People who share money freely share affection and love freely. I want to be generous, but that smacks against my fear. Between my desire for generosity and ingrained fears, I walk the tightrope of personality change.

Chapter 9
Sex

THE most intimate writing in recent years has come from women. Men, on the other hand, still believe in maintaining their male image. They have not discussed their emotions and pain publicly. I hope this book encourages other men to write about the collective pain we experience living in a patriarchal system that oppresses us almost as much as it does women.

I am a typically sexually obsessed American male—obsessed about performance, the size of my cock, competition, jealousy, and control. Like other American men, I feel I have to control the woman I am with. If she seems interested in another man, rage and fear roar through my body. Jealousy turns me into an irrational animal. I am always comparing myself sexually with other men.

In bed with my lover I lay the heaviest head trip of all on my body: How well am I *performing*?

This performance crisis centers around a point of basic male-female incompatibility: speed of climax. When the man comes, he comes. It lasts ten seconds maybe and afterward all sexual desire leaves you. It takes time to get excited again. Most women take longer to get excited, but they can come again and again.

Although I love to cuddle, kiss, eat, touch, and feel the closeness and the warmth of a woman's body, I have identified sex with performance. Because I have judged myself in bed and am scared that I may go soft, I have often avoided sexual contact.

For years I felt my cock was too small. Many American males think their cocks are not big enough. Bigness is sacred! A big cock means Big Business, and I have been overcompensating since childhood for what I thought was my small cock.

I created a Big Image. Whenever I arrived to give a speech in a college town, people who greeted me would often say, "We thought you were six feet tall." For years, while making love with women, I actually tried to hide my cock from sight. It took acrobatics, but it usually worked. The government may think I am a dangerous radical, but they don't know the true size of my cock!

I could never imagine my parents fucking. In fact,

I never saw my mother naked—her body was off-limits to me. Her tits were like the Treasure of Sierra Madre: touch them and die. My parents never discussed the subject of sex with me, nor were there suggestive books or pictures around the house. By the time I was a teenager they slept in separate beds. When the older guys in school told me about sex, I listened for groaning at night from my parents' bedroom, but I never heard a sound.

One of the most poignant moments of my life was when I visited my father in the hospital, where he was recovering from one of his heart attacks. Close to death, he was in a mood to review his life. "Mother refused to have sex with me," he said, and I could feel the pain in his body as he talked. Tears welled up in his eyes; his voice choked. "Mother kept saying she didn't want to because she was afraid that grandpa might hear the noise and get upset." I felt a rush of compassion for both my parents. My father had to put up with the tyranny of my grandfather, and sacrificed his desires to my mother's anxiety.

I also felt sympathy for my dead mother. Her father had smothered her with possessive love, putting her into a symbolic chastity belt. "Nobody can touch this but me," was his message to her. She learned from her mother that the role of woman is to be passive—to submit to a man when he desired sexual release, to bear his children, to serve his needs. No wonder my mother was so uninterested in sex. She had never been encouraged to enjoy it.

I rebelled against my parents outwardly, but I picked up their feelings about sex on an unconscious level. I remember the first day I masturbated. The feeling of my cock vibrating and sperm gushing from it was an intensely pleasurable release. But when it was over I felt guilty. It felt good but I wasn't supposed to feel that way. . . .

I feared that mother might know I was masturbating. What if she came in and found my hand on my cock? What explanation could I give, what excuse? So I masturbated quickly, trying to be as silent as hell. When it was over I dried the sperm with toilet paper. Sperm leaves a mark no matter how well you clean it up. Wouldn't mother see the soiled sheets? Well, maybe that is my silent secret with her. She knew and I knew, but nobody mentioned it.

During my teens I developed a masturbating pattern: imagine a girl from school, prop the pillow under my cock, rub it up a few times, let it come, and clean it up, all as quietly as possible. The quicker, the better. I had no interest in prolonging the erection. I was so ashamed of my cock that I didn't like to touch it. I had the opposite of penis envy: penis shame.

In high school I transferred much of my sex energy to writing about sports. I copied my father's busy-busy style. I never had time for sex. I masturbated quickly. I took girls to drive-in movies and rubbed myself on top of them or put their hand on my cock until I came in my pants. I loved to kiss and neck, and considered it a major victory when I got what we called "bare tit." Among the boys the big question was, "Did you get any?" If you didn't, you usually lied to maintain your reputation.

I felt sexually superior to women since I didn't think they enjoyed sex. If the man turned on, that was a woman's main satisfaction. I had no idea what female genitals were like. I felt lucky to be a man.

The first time I fucked with a woman, at twenty-two, she took my cock and stuck it in her pussy. I'm glad she did because I never would have found it myself. I came inside her and it felt cozy and complete, but still I thought, is that it?

My entire sexual history and masturbating pattern was training in premature ejaculation. If you come before or immediately upon entering, that's premature. I often found it hard to contain the initial rush of excitement.

I felt so sorry at coming quickly that I repressed my enjoyment of orgasm. I began to prefer masturbation to fucking. In masturbating, I experienced explosive, dynamic orgasms throughout my entire body. In fucking, I felt shame and failure when I came quickly. And when I didn't get it up, I felt like a worm.

I used to wonder if I was laying this trip on myself or responding to my partner's demands. I concluded that it was me—I had huge self-expectations of what it means to be a man. Instead of enjoying my climax, I felt guilty and even tried to hide the fact that I was coming.

At times I have had trouble getting it up. My cock does not always heed my mind. I can't say when it's going to be hard or soft. Sometimes I feel very turned on and my cock stays neutral. Other times it's hard as a rock. Sometimes I feel that I have cycles.

Most men act so tough and strong on the outside, putting on a big show of masculinity. Why? Because on the inside we are scared, weak, and fragile. Men, not women, are the weaker sex. We are scared of not performing, of being "limp," even when we are not.

Women have been discussing frigidity for years; men don't even like to mention the word "impotence."

Jerry Rubin

Going limp is the most emasculating experience of a man's life.

How can I describe to women the pain and agony a man feels when he does not get it up, when he feels because his cock is soft that he is not A MAN?

We have defined manhood as making money, doing well in sports, fucking a lot of women. We think it so important to win that we constantly con each other. We don't let the truth out that we are vulnerable. We see ourselves as competitive athletes fighting for the rewards of life—women, status, money, power. We need women to tell us that we are men.

My father taught me a lot about competition in sports, but little about pleasure-sharing. As a kid my uncles put boxing gloves on my cousin and me, and forced us to hit each other for their benefit. I learned to express aggression and defend myself, but not to express and accept affection.

Men have been conditioned from birth to apply the sports example to all situations in our life: the bedroom is seen as a continuation of the gymnasium. Women become the object; other men the enemy. And at the end it is: What's the score? Did you win or lose?

As a political activist in the sixties, I created a macho image of toughness and violence to impress women and hide my weakness. I wanted to *appear* as ferocious as the men in the Pentagon I was attacking. People were often shocked to meet me. "You're so sweet and gentle," they said.

Thanks to the example set by women, men in America are starting to re-examine the concept of manhood, looking for a new definition of masculinity that incorporates both sensitivity and vulnerability. My women friends and lovers have given me space to be less of a "man" and more me.

I overcame my body shyness through experience in the growth movement and learning from women. I wish I could learn about sex from other men. But men avoid intimate conversations about sex. Outside of men's consciousness groups, our pattern of conversation is locked in the locker rooms.

When I went to see Stanley Goldman, the bioenergetic therapist, I told him that I was embarrassed about the size of my cock. Stanley suggested that I announce to the woman I'm with, "Is it big enough for you? Take charge of the situation, Jerry! Don't condemn yourself, don't live in shame, don't hide from yourself."

In reducing my obsession with sex, I am developing a new relationship with my cock. I love it, and my entire masculinity is not bound up in my cock. I no longer need to relate to women solely through it.

Studying massage helped break my shyness about my body. Doing massage, we looked at each other's genitals and massaged each other. Nakedness and touching felt natural; there was no sense of shame or judgment. Men and women massaged my body, including my genitals, and I massaged other peoples' bodies. Everything felt good!

I went through the weirdest changes while massaging a sixty-year-old man. His body felt good; it felt nice to run my hands over it; his age and sex made no difference. Some men felt smooth and soft; some women firm and strong. Massage taught me that touch is the most important aspect of sexual pleasure.

I realized how tight and tense certain parts of my body are; how painful it felt to have my legs massaged with a soft stroke. As my partner massaged my legs, I tensed up, nervous, I wanted him to stop. This brought me directly up against my fear of pleasure.

In the fall of 1974 I decided to see a sex therapist because I was worried about the way I was swinging from overexcitement to noninterest in sex. My sex surrogate turned out to be a pretty, pug-nosed blonde woman named Sue who worked at the rate of $115 for three hours, the third hour being spent in conversation with a male co-therapist.

I drove to her house in Berkeley, and we talked for twenty minutes. She seemed as nervous as I felt. She offered me some wine which I refused. She told me she had to confront her own personal doubts about being a sex surrogate to assure herself that it was not a sophisticated form of prostitution. After we talked, she said that she felt better, but she still seemed slightly apologetic.

We both showered and went into the bedroom. I climbed into a large double bed and watched her as she shed her robe and dried herself. Her face was radiant yet sheepish. I immediately relaxed. Sue was a soft person. She smiled whimsically as she climbed into bed and offered me a joint. I accepted.

We did spoon breathing, in which one partner holds the other from behind and the couple breathes together. But while we were breathing, I felt my mind wander. I can tolerate pain, but in sex I confront my fear of pleasure. In fact, conflict brings out the best in me because I am used to a confrontation. But when pleasure comes, I feel I don't deserve it. In bed I am a performance machine; sex becomes a new form of work. What the hell. Sex is fun or fuck it. (And why aren't I focusing on my breathing?)

We massaged each other for two hours, breathing together. I wanted to learn to receive as well as give, to allow rather than control. Sexual excitement is primarily a form of breathing control, to spread the energy throughout my body, rather than to locate it all in my genitals.

Sue suggested long hot baths in which I put all attention on my breathing and feel the energy streaming throughout my body, and one-hour self-massage masturbation sessions in which I enjoy my erection, rather than giving in to immediate release.

I used to be ashamed of masturbating, but the women's movement liberated my feelings about it. An entire literature teaching women how to masturbate for pleasure has grown up. So why not men?

Sue suggested masturbation as a beginning cure to sexual "problems." Long all-body self-massages, kissing, rubbing and feeling my own body, are preparations for enhanced lovemaking with another. And if someone calls, I say, "Can't talk to you now—I'm masturbating."

My experience with sex therapy and later with women helped turn my head and body around. The goal of sex is not orgasm. In fact, the best sex has no goal other than for every moment to be an end-in-itself. Maintaining an erection for as long as possible sustains sex energy. Breathing into my cock and feeling energy throughout my system is inspiring.

I took the advice of the sex surrogate and started giving myself long massages. I lay in bed, touched my body all over, wetting and kissing myself. While I was doing this, my internal demon kept trying to make me feel guilty, calling me an egomaniac for giving myself pleasure. My demon was torturing me. Once I realized that my demon was educated in masochism and puritanism, I began to stop taking it so seriously. My demon makes sex an obsession by making such a *special* thing about it.

The demon that lives within each of us can be countered only if it is recognized and identified. My demon is my programming, and I meet it most clearly while masturbating. That act angers my parents-in-me more than anything else. And you know the weird thing—my real parents probably wouldn't even mind! It's my parents-in-me that are complaining!

I love to watch women move, observe their curves and grace. I love to watch them laugh. I love to imagine a beautiful woman in bed with me, taking off her clothes, piece by piece. I love to feel a warm female hand rubbing up and down my legs. I love the loss of self-consciousness that takes place with exciting sex. I love to kiss, to send my tongue deep into my lover's mouth. I love to sweat, let go. I love to lie in bed naked and giggle together.

Many articles on sex today ask whether the new women's consciousness of rising sexual expectations is increasing male impotence. Reports of impotency are more frequent, but that may reflect a new honesty, rather than a response to the New Woman. But the women's movement does create an immediate problem because of its own contradictions.

Women, however liberated they are, are not free of male chauvinism when they look to a man to prove to them they are a woman. A woman who considered herself a feminist cried when I did not get a hard-on. My neutral cock pushed her "I-am-not-beautiful, I-am-a-failure" buttons. She felt that my soft cock exposed my lack of passion for her. Truth is, I felt very turned-on, and it was painful for me to have nothing happening with my cock. But no explanation made her feel better. She cried.

I slept a number of times with another woman who, out of bed, proclaimed her independence from men. In bed she wanted to be overwhelmed by a powerful man and made to submit. She said that no matter how liberated, every woman at some level desires to be overpowered by a man she loves. This little girl in every woman, the programmed, emotional child, feeds into the male chauvinist view of sex as conquest.

To the extent that some liberated women are looking for That Great Big Cock In The Sky to give them multiple orgasms, liberated women are male chauvinists in drag, using men for their self-approval, demanding that men perform well.

As women free themselves from male-indoctrinated conditioning, their increased consciousness will liberate sex. Women enjoy touching, feeling, taking time to spread sexual feelings all over the body. I have learned from women to see sex as a total act, not just genital contact.

I am enjoying the fact too that the new women's consciousness means women are beginning to pursue men. When women call me on the phone to ask me out, it makes me feel desired. I get turned on by women who are independent individuals; those who are appendages to men bore me.

In sex, anything goes. The emphasis on genitals, orgasm, and performance comes from a puritan society that encourages goal-directed behavior. In my emphasis on orgasm, I carried capitalistic values into bed with me. No wonder I often lost interest in sex. Sex as athletics is a struggle. But going into bed to smell, taste, touch, feel, relax, enjoy makes sex pure pleasure.

I am afraid of naked sexual contact with men. I love men as much as I love women, yet I never think of physically satisfying and being satisfied by men. Men do not turn me on because I was propagandized as a child to think that homosexuality is sick.

When I was sixteen, my favorite high school teacher and I went on a trip to visit colleges. We slept in the same room, and he spent the night trying to seduce me. After a while he fell asleep, but I stayed awake all night, fearful that he might jump in my bed and rape me. The next morning we both tried to act as if nothing had happened.

When we got home I told my parents and they were very upset. We considered taking the information to school authorities, but I loved the teacher too much. A few weeks later he called me into his office and apologized for the incident.

During my one year at Oberlin College a male friend and I wrote anonymous letters to a senator saying that another friend was a homosexual. He wasn't, but what a laugh we would have when literature on homosexuality arrived from the senator's office at our friend's mailbox! The senator, however, sent my letters back to the university, which launched an exhaustive search through the dormitories until they found our typewriter. Even though we explained it was just a joke, the university officials kicked us out of school for two weeks and cancelled my scholarship. To call someone a homosexual obviously was a serious insult.

I myself aided in the legal harassment of homosexuals. One night, when I was seventeen, a man in the Cincinnati Public Library wrote me a note proposing to meet me in the bathroom the next Friday. I went to the vice squad of the Cincinnati Police Department and together we set a trap for the guy. The cops caught him, threatened him, and let him go. I watched the whole thing, thinking that I had captured some criminal.

In *Do It!* I described homosexuality as sick. The gay community attacked me publicly, forcing me for the first time to examine my sexual bias. I began to see that I had been a victim of the American sexual lie against homosexuality. Sex between two men or two women (or three) is as human as male-female sex.

The thought of two men fucking still scares me, maybe because of my antihomosexual upbringing. To make love with a man would be like making love with a mirror image of myself, a legitimate aspect of general sexual self-pleasure. I now embrace, touch, and kiss men on the lips. I enjoy kissing and holding male friends, but I have never become turned on to a man's genitals.

Sex is sex, and nothing more. There is no need to make the act symbolic of one's manhood. Whenever sex gets troublesome, it's not worth it. Sex is a place for fun and pleasure.

At thirty-seven I am learning things about sex that I wished I had learned as a child. I thought as I grew older, my sexual interests or capacities might decrease, but in truth both have increased with increasing awareness. I enjoy watching a woman get turned on by my body. It's a turn-on for me to feel the changes in her breathing and her body flow. I love to express tenderness, softness, closeness, and sensitivity, and feel the same. In sex I become the animal I really am.

It's important for me to learn to communicate honestly in bed with my lover. We are in bed to give pleasure to each other, so it is natural for each partner to say, "Touch me here, I like it this way." After sex it is fun to share experiences. It's colossal the amount of misunderstanding that goes on in bed. Talking openly about sex solves most of the problems.

I am discovering my natural balance of sexuality, which means not laying a "you must" trip on myself; discovering my true interests, my real rhythm. I am becoming less of a sexual obsessive, and putting sex in its proper place. As Sam Keen writes: "Sex is best when it is not important."

Chapter 10

Can a Las Vegas Gambler Save My Life?

HE swamis say that you don't have to find your teacher; when you are ready, your teacher will find you. In January, 1974, I was attending a Consciousness Festival in San Francisco—two days of talks and demonstrations of everything from biofeedback to tantric yoga and astrology—when I wandered into an introductory lecture of Fischer-Hoffman Psychic Therapy.

Immediately I was turned off. The man giving the presentation wore a green suit and brown-white-red shoes. He sounded like a used-car salesman, and his sales tactics—high pressure, fantastic claims, and guarantees—made me think, "Jesus, fast-buck hustlers have gotten into the therapy business." When he told the thirty-five people in the room that the cost was $500, three-fourths of the room emptied out en masse. I stayed to ask some questions about this "psychic therapy."

The man said that psychic therapy "cured" people of their hang-ups by reversing the negative programming of childhood. All your hang-ups, he said, came from your mother and father during the first thirteen years of your life. "How does this miraculous reversal of conditioning take place?" I asked. He spoke mysteriously of "spirit guides" and emotionally cathartic experiences; weekly group sessions where nobody talks to each other; and lectures on video tape by the therapy's founder, ex-suit salesman Bob Hoffman. Then you go home and do the actual work yourself, quantities of writing, until at the end of fourteen weeks you have compiled a book-length emotional autobiography. I kept raising my hand and asking questions: "How does this work where other therapies fail?" But the man gave no direct answers. "Experience it and find out," he said.

The whole trip sounded like a fraud. My college-educated intellect rebelled at the nonintellectual style of the man in the green suit. Yet I'd heard that Claudio Naranjo, a psychoanalyst and gestalt therapist, thought so highly of the therapy that he had asked everybody in his Seekers After Truth, S.A.T., Berkeley's largest spiritual and meditation organization, to take it as a basic emotional housecleaning. And a professor of psychology at the University of California called it the "therapy of the future." My intellect found what it needed to confirm the decision I had already made intuitively—to pay my $500 and try psychic therapy.

The aspect of psychic therapy that most appealed to me was its fourteen-week time limit. No going to a therapist once a week for ten years. This therapy combines various theories and techniques into an intense short-order package and works with American business efficiency!

To my dismay, however, the therapy's offices were located in the heart of downtown Oakland—across the street from the Oakland *Tribune,* one of the most reactionary newspapers in America! Eight years earlier I had gone to the Oakland *Tribune* to picket their racist hiring practices. Now I was returning to that same corner to discover my essence!

What was I doing? Here was Jerry Rubin—famous radical, liberated personality, threat to the United States government—entering a therapy institution, admitting he was neurotic. I expected the therapists to exploit the situation, to try to "prove" that my political activities were also neurotic. I imagined them saying behind my back: "All he was really doing in those riots of the 1960's was attacking his parents; it was just an adolescent rebellion." So I became supersensitive to any political slights. A couple of times other clients looked at my name tag—we all wore name tags—and asked, "You're not THE Jerry Rubin are you?" I shook my head no. If I had said yes, people might have responded with, "I thought you would be out blowing up buildings!" or "What are YOU doing HERE?" or "Gee, you sure have changed."

Guess who became my therapist? The Man in the

125

Green Suit. His name was Dick Russell, and one of the first things he told me was that he believed that napalmed babies were burning off their own karma from past lives. I raged inside when I heard this vicious racism in the name of spirituality, but I kept quiet. In the past I would have tongue-lashed this person, making him feel like shit, and then stormed out of the room, slamming the door behind.

My mellowing enabled me to hear my therapist's reactionary politics and stay on. I felt inside that he had something I wanted—badly. I had come to psychic therapy to find the person I had been searching for all my life—me.

The irony of finding myself in a therapy to learn to love my parents tickled me because it was only five years earlier that the *National Enquirer* ran a fearsome front-page picture of me angrily pointing my finger under the headline: YIPPIE LEADER TELLS CHILDREN TO KILL THEIR PARENTS.

The idea for "Kill Your Parents" came to me when I heard someone say, "Anyone who is not willing to kill his parents for the revolution is not a revolutionary." That statement appealed to me. Not that I thought it was practical unless your father is Adolf Hitler, but I saw it as a basic statement of psychological commitment. Are you willing to give up your attachments for total change, or are you a "yes, but" revolutionary?

As I went from campus to campus in the late 1960's giving speeches, slogans like "Smash ROTC" and "Burn Down Your College" gradually lost their impact. After a while even the most radical statements turned to mush. But when I said "Kill Your Parents" everybody woke up, shocked. A few hardy malcontents even stood

up and cheered. Most looked at me in stunned silence,
"Does he mean that *literally*?" "Kill Your Parents"
became the perfect statement for getting people to
confront themselves instantly.

But five years later, I finally understood what I
meant! Kill the *parents-in-you*.

In the sixties I was trying to break the chain of conditioning that perpetuates negative programming. "Kill
Your Parents" was said to shock people into a new
consciousness about their ability to re-create themselves. It didn't work because people took the word
"kill" literally. In 1974, at the age of thirty-six, after
my parents had been dead for fourteen years, I began
to purge them from me. I carried out internally what
I advocated externally in the sixties.

How do I learn to kill the parents-in-me?

"Ask your spirit guide," says psychic therapy.

Spirit guide? What the hell was Dick Russell talking
about?

Again I was suspicious and wanted to get out.

"There is a spirit world above us," Russell said, "in-
habited by spirits without bodies. All of us have spirits
who watch over us, love us, tell us the truth, but most
people do not listen to their spirits."

Our assignment was to make contact with our spirit
guide. Most people in the group found their spirit
guides rather painlessly on their own. I resisted. I have
never believed in any world beyond the physical world.
If there were spirit guides, science would find them.
Besides, I closed my eyes and nobody came knocking.

Dick took me into a small room and asked me to
close my eyes and imagine a blue sky. "See a white
disk coming down," he said, "and now see behind the

127

disk eyes, a mouth, a chin, a neck, a stomach, a body.
. . . Describe the person you see."

I saw nothing.

"Try again," Dick said. "Your guide is there in the
sky waiting for an invitation to come down. Your guide
may be male or female, young or old. As soon as you
contact your guide, you will never lose contact again."

"Can my guide be my friend Stew?" I asked.

"No," Dick said. "Your guide is not a person on the
earth plane. Your guide is a spirit."

I closed my eyes again and imagined a black man,
tall and strong, trying perhaps to project my image of
the Black Revolutionary onto the spirit world. "If you
distrust the guide, it's not your guide," said Dick. "Walk
up to the black man and try to pull off his face. What
happens?"

I pulled his face and it came off like a mask. But
underneath the mask was another face. I saw deep
blue eyes, a round face, long blonde hair, a plump
body, an enormous presence. A female voice spoke,
"Hello, Jerry, I'm your guide who has come from
another plane of reality to help you."

"Ask your guide her name," Dick said.

I did.

"Lorraine," she answered.

Had I invented a Big Jewish Mama in the sky to
help me? Wasn't this a big put-on, or was there really
a Lorraine up there just waiting for me to call her?
I felt her presence. Warmth filled my entire body. I
even felt Lorraine's arms around me.

"Lorraine sounds like the mother I never had," I
said, "or maybe even a replacement for Rhoda."

"You're projecting your needs onto Lorraine," Dick

said. "Lorraine is real, not an invention or projection. We always get the spirit guide we need to help us evolve spiritually at each step in our lives. At this moment you need a living mother. When you no longer do, Lorraine will leave and you will find another guide for your next evolutionary step."

Dick got up and left, and I sat there. I had the strange feeling that I was no longer alone. Lorraine was there too, watching me, aware of my thoughts and feelings, living with me from the inside. I felt her love.

"I don't believe in spirits, Lorraine," I said. "You don't exist and I am just fooling myself."

"I am here as long as you want me and believe in me," Lorraine replied. "I am here to serve you because I love you."

"Lorraine, you're a hallucination! This therapy has got me talking to myself! Talking to spirits! What are my revolutionary buddies going to think now? Jerry Rubin has gone crazy!"

Suddenly a feeling came over me. I felt it bubble in my stomach and rise to my head, filling my consciousness. It was the same feeling I had experienced as a child.

I was home, hiding in the bathroom after a screaming fight with my mother. After I had locked myself in, a voice whispered to me: "Jerry, you do not have to be this way. You don't have to fight. You can be above all this." I knew that the voice was me—but an unfamiliar part of me, and it scared me. As the voice talked on, I heard another part of me scream: SHUT UP! Five minutes later my mother and I were yelling at each other again and I heaved my lunch—a plate full of tuna fish—on the floor to prove that I was boss.

Occasionally during my childhood, in the middle of an emotional uproar, that quiet voice would return. "Jerry, you can get everything you want in life by being lovable. You do not have to scream and shout to get your way." Once I actually listened to that voice and acted on it. In the middle of a fight I melted my mother with my look of love. "What's come over you?" she asked, astonished. The fight evaporated. My mother smiled. "Why can't you be like this all the time?" she asked. But an hour later I slammed the door in my mother's face again, calling her a "goddamn bitch," and I jumped sulkily into bed.

Has my spirit guide really been with me all my life? I know that I have always been aware of "two voices" within me, the voice of ego and the voice of truth. Was the spirit guide the voice of truth?

I flashed back to the 1960's and my radical career. At times ego and ambition drove me on, but I was also sincerely concerned about poor people, suffering, inequality, injustice. My love of people and my willingness to sacrifice my life for others sometimes even surprised me. Was my spirit guide silently with me in the 1960's directing my behavior so that my ego didn't overdominate me?

Still I wasn't satisfied; I needed to explain what was happening to me in psychological, scientific terms. I got it! Within each of us, beyond our programming, exists a higher self. Lorraine is my higher self!

I decided to ask Lorraine. "Are you my higher self, Lorraine?" I asked. "Call me whatever you want," she said. "The name doesn't make any difference. Consider me your healthy alter ego if you like, or your teacher, your source of strength. The important thing is that you use me. Whenever you are in an emotional conflict, call on me. I will help guide you through psychic therapy, and aid you in your evolution."

The skeptic in me still suspected the psychic part of psychic therapy. The rest of the therapy, though, seemed quite familiar. It was a casserole of techniques and insights from everyone: Freud, Janov, Maslow, Perls, Berne, Seth, Don Juan, Jung. The foundation of the therapy is similar to Eric Berne's Transactional Analysis. The emphasis on childhood comes from Freud. The conversations between different parts of yourself is similar to gestalt. Reichian, bioenergetic, and primal techniques are used. And the overall philosophy is an outgrowth of Eastern spirituality.

Once a week I went to a group meeting where we were guided collectively through processes which were experienced on a personal basis. Then I went home and worked alone for fifteen to twenty hours a week on the homework exercises—emotional assignments that had to be written up or taped. I sent the homework to my therapist so he could check to see if it was gut-level, emotionally deep and complete, and if I was ready to go on to the next session.

I kept looking for reasons to drop out of the therapy. At first I was put off by all this talk of how Bob Hoffman received the therapy from the living spirit of a dead psychiatrist. Then I realized that if it works, it doesn't make any difference how Hoffman says he got it. Dr. Siegfried Fischer, an Oakland psychiatrist, died in 1966. Six months later, Bob says, he was suddenly awakened in the middle of the night to "see" the spirit of Dr. Fischer at the foot of his bed.

"Go away, I have to sleep," Bob said.

"Wait, Bob, I must talk to you," Fischer said. "I know now that you were right: when the body dies the mind goes on. Now that I am on this side, I also know why psychiatry has failed. Now that I am here, I have a method that works."

"Great, so what do you want from me?" Bob replied, wanting to go back to sleep.

"I need a channel to bring this method to the world," said Dr. Fischer.

"Me?" asked Hoffman incredulously. "I'm only a tailor. Who's going to listen to me?"

That night the spirit of Dr. Fischer took Hoffman through a primitive form of what became the Fischer-Hoffman Psychic Therapy process. "My brains were blown," recalls Bob. "In one night I learned through Dr. Fischer how to love myself and others selflessly, how to give to give rather than give to get. Dr. Fischer freed me of my parents by evoking in me compassion, forgiveness, and love for them." Hoffman became a channel for Dr. Fischer, reporting to other people what he said.

The theory of psychic therapy is that after our physical death our spirit goes to a level consistent with the karma it achieved on the earth plane. We return, in new bodies, to continue working out our karma. Karma results from positive or negative behavior on the earth. Past, present, and future coexist simultaneously, and you can tune into the proper vibrations to see any plane. The mind never dies.

"We choose our parents," says Bob Hoffman, "in order to get the karmic problems we need to advance to the next level of consciousness and freedom. We are not victims because we choose everything that happens to us in our lifetime, including our parents."

"We select our parents?"
I nearly choked over that one.
Contacting Lorraine again was not easy for me. I repressed her because I felt that I did not deserve her. But soon I began to develop techniques to get in touch with her. First I learned to distrust my first reaction of fear and insecurity. Then I learned to put my consciousness in the pit of my stomach. Lorraine lived there. "Get in touch with me as a bubble deep in your gut," she said. "Forget your head, even distrust your feelings. Direct your awareness to your stomach and imagine a big ocean. Then see me bubble out of the water and float up to your consciousness. Listen to me even though what I say will often be painful, because it will go against what your ego believes. I am not here to tell you what you want to hear. Your ego does that for you. I am here to tell you the truth, to put you in harmony with life. Remember, Jerry, you are going to get what you want, whether you want it or not."

My father once called me my own worst enemy, because I was so impatient and never appreciated what I got. Now Lorraine was saying the same things. "Jerry, your ego is a devil out to sacrifice the present to protect the past. Your ego comes from your conditioning and holds onto the past. If you let your ego direct your life, you will never live in the moment and be happy. But I don't want to talk abstractly to you. You can spend your entire life in abstract argument, and never change. You have to *do* something to free yourself from your conditioning."

By locating Lorraine in my body, I was finding within myself a secure place, a nurturing center. It was not a head trip. I was directing my energy and my awareness to particular places in my body. To do this

133

I usually had to change my breathing. That alone brought psychological relief to tense situations. Eventually the feeling of Lorraine came to me without closing my eyes or directing my awareness. The voice of Lorraine became integrated into my being.

One day while writing this book I suddenly perceived myself as an open channel—an empty system through which energy flows. If I unclog and open up my system, I can allow energy to flow unimpeded through my mind and body. I had the eerie feeling that I was not even writing my book. I flashed on something Bob Dylan once said, "I didn't write any of my songs. They flowed through me. I am a channel."

"Trying" blocks the energy flow. All I have to do is stop trying, sit enough hours at the typewriter, and let the words flow through me. Write from my stomach, rather than from my head. Keep my ego out of it. Let the book write itself.

Ecstatic with this discovery, I ran to the phone to call Dick Russell. But before I got him on the phone, Lorraine stopped me. "If you talk about it too much, Jerry, you will lose it," she said. "Stop turning ideas into objects. The important thing is to embody it, be it, do it. Don't let your ego capture these new insights and turn them into triumphs for the ego. Watch out for that ego of yours. He's huge, tough, stubborn, strong. He'll fight for victory and call it spirituality."

Chapter 11

I Can't Be Relaxed in an Anxious Womb

HE unusual aspect of psychic therapy was writing down my innermost fears and feelings on paper. What follows in this chapter are entries into my psychic therapy diary.

The first psychic therapy assignment was to list my mother's and father's negative traits and the negative messages they communicated to me. I came up with thirty. My therapist ordered me to do the assignment again, and this time to see my parents as they really were, not as I wanted them to be. I didn't want to believe that my parents were *that* bad. They loved me, fed me, clothed me, sent me to good schools, took care of me. How could I be so ungrateful?

Dick gave me a list of fifteen hundred possible negative traits and admonitions. If something on the list resonated in my gut, I checked it. I was no longer trying to please my parents. Two hours later I had checked 240 negative traits and 220 negative admonitions from mother and 285 negative traits and 197 admonitions from father.

I was taking my mother and father off their pedestals! I had in front of me a map of the negative imprinting I had picked up from my parents. The point was obvious—I did not invent or create my negativity, I adopted it. I went over each trait and message to see if I had that trait today in my adult life. The result was shocking: at the age of thirty-seven I was practically a carbon copy of my dead mother and father.

At one of our weekly sessions people sat hunched over in their chairs, anger and pain visible in their faces. Spread over the room were pillows, belts, straps, boxing gloves, punching bags, plastic baseball bats. To a veteran of the antiwar movement of the sixties, this felt a little like Lincoln Park in Chicago before the police tear gas, or Telegraph Avenue in Berkeley before a riot. But the people here had not come together to attack the Bank of America or throw rocks at cops. We were here to rip our parents to shreds, tear them limb from limb, knock out their teeth, gouge out their eyes, and leave their bloody bodies hanging from the nearest tree.

We lay on pillows and mats, thinking emotion-releasing sentences from our childhood deprivation:

"Mommy, don't leave me." Saying it over and over again to ourselves and breathing heavily in-and-out until we felt lightheaded. Oxygen filled our bodies, energy radiated from our heads. Growing dizzy, we wanted to stop. But, no—that was the time to press on, moving our eyes up and down, then side to side, turning our heads quickly, kicking our feet wildly, shaking up the body blocks, mechanical movements which stimulated deep gut-level feelings. Over and over again we cried out, "Daddy, don't leave me alone." Repressed feelings would overcome us as we contacted our deepest pain. Forty- and fifty-year-olds, in fetal and baby postures, cried, sobbed, reached their infant arms out, crying, "Please, Mommy, please . . . hold me . . ."

Therapists moving around the room were shouting, "Daddy was not there for you!" "Mommy hated you!" The sobbing and crying intensified; a room full of pained, screaming children.

The therapists picked up each bawling baby, one by one, holding him in their arms, rocking him back and forth, giving him the comfort and security that mommy and daddy never gave. "You're a little boy who wants love. You deserve love. It's O.K. to feel. It's O.K. to cry."

We started a bioenergetic exercise of standing, tilting backward, breathing deeply and screaming at the top of our lungs. Within minutes people were sweating, kicking, screaming, crying, punching, pounding, becoming wild animals, beating their mothers and fathers to a pulp.

When anyone stopped screaming, three therapists were right there to scream the person back into fury: "Don't stop! Hit that bitch for the first time in your life!

Express the anger you have held in all your life! HIT HER AGAIN!" This bitch session is a declaration of independence. It emotionally shocks the unconscious of the body. It is an act of self-love. I have to love myself to want to be free from my parents.

Lorraine brings into my mind's eye the spirit of my mother and father kicking and screaming. She ties their arms and legs to a tree with steel, and gags them with a thick rope so they cannot move or make a sound. Then I start shouting at my mother for the specific messages she gave me.

"Thanks, Mommy. You white-skinned no-good sexless asshole cap-toothed cancerous venom of a snake who destroyed me from birth. Why didn't you just suffocate me instead of killing me like you did? You taught me to hate myself, to feel guilty, to drive myself crazy, to turn my anger against myself, to turn my energy off, to hate my body, to hate women. I hate myself because I am you. I want to die to kill the Mommy inside me. I hate what you taught me:

'DON'T BE LOVED'

"You didn't want me. I was born into the world in the body of a woman who did not want me. No wonder I feel so needy, fearful, so thankful for everything I get, because I know in my gut that my mother—the most important person to me in my life—did not want me. Did you kiss me? Hold me? No, you never let your body touch mine! I am so anxious, so nervous about touching others. You scarred me for life. No wonder I reject women before they can reject me; no wonder I want to possess and suffocate women! Because you cheated me at birth. YOU CHEAT!

'BE DEPENDENT ON MOMMY'

"Remember how you kept me dependent on you by doing everything for me. I am still that little, dependent child. I kept myself small, so I could stay a little boy, dependent on you, you asshole. I have not deserted you by becoming mature or happy or getting someone else's love. If I get someone else to love me I will not need you, Mommy, and you want me to need you.

"I am afraid to be alone, because when I am alone I hear your voice inside me. There is nothing inside me but your boredom, your anxiety, your fears. I always ran out of the house to be away from you. But I can never run away from you. The more I hate you, the more I must hate myself because your bad breath is my breath, your white skin is my skin, your piano legs are my piano legs, your body blocks are my body blocks, you are me and I am you and that's why I hate myself because I HATE YOU! You bitch!

'JUDGE EVERYONE YOU MEET'

"I have your self-righteous right-wrong should-should-not programming. Here I am, just like you, asshole Mommy, judging people. Feeling superior, me up and others down, building walls around myself, with that stupid JUDGE inside me that I got from you. I don't see people as they are, but as they fit to my standards, my self-righteous beliefs.

"I hate my belief that I have the only truth and that everyone else is wrong. I hate my salesman's attitude that I must sell because that is the only way to relate to people, the only way to define myself.

Jerry Rubin

'LIVE ON GUILT'

"I took your bullshit about being a victim, oppressed by two thousand years of suffering, and built myself a political trip full of self-righteousness. I became an orthodox Jewish yippie rabbi with heavy morality trips JUST LIKE YOU MOMMY except that I did it rebelliously, spitting in your face. Yes, Mommy, I made a fool of you in public. I got even with you. My only regret is that you did not stay alive long enough to see me make a name for myself attacking all the things you taught me.

'WHEN IN DOUBT, WORRY'

"You used to sit and do nothing all day but worry. So I worry. When you died worry was put to sleep. I am glad you died. Yes, I can say it now! I wanted revenge for what you did to me. I wish you would have suffered even more pain than you did because you deserve it. Oh, it is so liberating for me to tell the truth. MOMMY I AM GLAD THAT YOU DIED. IF YOU HAD NOT DIED OF CANCER, I WOULD HAVE HAD TO KILL YOU.

"First you robbed me of my security, and then you taught me to cope with coldness through worry and anxiety, you mistress of boredom!

'COMPARE AND COMPETE'

"Remember how you compared me to my cousins. And to my own brother! You told me that I was a bad

140

boy and Gil was a good boy! You taught me to compete and compare, to fear and outdo. I became a ferocious achievement-oriented, compulsive, obsessive, live-in-my-head asshole, happy when others did bad because it made me feel superior.

"Since I do not love myself, I am mistrustful when other people like me. Since, like you, I am empty, I am only out for myself and everyone is my competitor and potential enemy. You child killer, child molester, child murderer—cancerous BEAST!!!!

'HATE WOMEN'

"Every woman I see is no good—too tall, too short, not Jewish, not smart, not this, not that. I have a million excuses because I am scared of women. When I find one I like, I drive her crazy with my neediness, anxiety, possessiveness. You taught me to hate women, Mommy. You, sexless lifeless castrating energy-draining, are my model for all women!

"I am doing to all women what I would like to do to you. I make them pay for my hatred toward you. I want to fail with women to prove to you that NO OTHER WOMAN WILL TAKE YOUR PLACE! Now will you love me? If I am happy, I will be betraying your teachings. And then you will be jealous, and won't love me. Well fuck you, Mommy, fuck you in the ass with a red-hot poker and let your arms and legs fall off and leave you in the middle of the road run over by the meanest car I ever saw."

And then I saw my father bound and gagged, and I went up to him and began screaming:

141

Jerry Rubin

SEE ALL MEN AS ME

"You son of a bitch, you shit-face. I've gone through life fearing men, turning my male friends into fathers because my father was a little kid who ran around the house threatening people. Where is the soft, gentle, and loving man? Where is the man who gives his wife a supportive, loving environment, an understanding heart, a soul full of appreciation?

'BE WEAK INSIDE—TOUGH OUTSIDE'

"I hate your combination of weakness and tyranny. Inside the house you called me a bad boy, but outside all you did was brag about me. You wanted me to give you feelings of importance. Your bluster and threatening behavior hides your incredible neediness. To think you are my male model! The essence of maleness: *bluster on the outside, zero on the inside.* And I have gone through my life blustering and running. I learned from you that image is more important than reality. Remember how you used to put your foot down? Well here is my foot on your head. Crunch, crunch. Remember how you used to teach me a lesson? Well here is a lesson for you in the teeth.

'USE FORCE TO GET YOUR WAY'

"What a temper! You used your goddamn temper, your mean voice, and your incredible anger to control me. You were always physically threatening me, weren't you? Big man—to push a kid around. Child

142

beater! I had to keep away from you because I was so goddamn scared of you. You wanted me to jump when you barked. Well, fuck you, asshole. You'll jump when I bark! Remember when you phoned me from work to tell me that I was going to 'get it' when you got home? I was scared to death, I paced the house in fear of what my father, my own father, was going to do to me. I lived in fucking fear of you.

'HURRY! HURRY! HURRY!'

"You did everything so bloody fast. You ate your goddamn food in three minutes flat. Before anyone else in the family had a chance to take a bite, you wolfed it all down. You never even tasted your food. You woke up to eat so you could shit so you could go back to sleep to wake up to eat to shit. Eat and shit, eat and shit. Fast, fast, fast. You were in a hurry to go to your grave.

'NEED AND REJECT WOMEN'

"You went through your life looking for a woman who would reject you. You reject and she rejects. What a stupid wasteful game. You could have made mother so happy and brought out her beauty, her softness, her femininity, but instead you put her on a pedestal, and masochistically enjoyed sacrificing your life to hers. And then what did you do? Bastard father! What did you do? As soon as Mommy got sick, you gave yourself a heart attack. 'If my wife dies, I die too.' You did. You abandoned Gil and me. You spent your whole life leaving us. You were always packing your bags, threat-

Jerry Rubin

ening to leave, and that's why I fear that people I'm with will leave me and why I always threaten to leave them first. You gave me my 'abandonment button.'

'LIVE IN YOUR IMAGE'

"You taught me to live for image and not for reality. You, Daddy, taught me that my reputation, what other people think of me, my image, being famous, is more important than living a deep, warm, intimate, personal life in which I satisfy myself. Inside I don't love myself. So I have to seek from the outside world proof that I really am a good guy after all.

"Hands up, Father. This is a stickup. I am robbing you of your shit. I am going to stick my knife right into your stomach and make you feel the pain I have felt."

After this group session we went home and spent a week bitching at our internalized parents. Meanwhile, we had no contact with our living parents. To bitch at them in person would destroy the process. We are freeing ourselves, not punishing them, attacking the parents-in-us, not our breathing parents.

My anger was blocked at first. All I could say was, "I'm sorry, mother, I'm sorry." I blamed myself for my mother's sickness and death. Then I wrote the sentence that freed me: "Mommy, goddamn you, I am glad that you died of cancer. If you had not died, I would have had to kill you." I had released my deepest childhood fears. I said the worst and nothing happened! I was not struck dead by God! My therapist had encouraged and supported my feelings and given me permission to hate my mother; my child within was not guilty or evil.

Screaming at mother and father in the bitch sessions made me feel better because for the first time in my life I stopped blaming myself for being a bad boy. I blamed my parents. That was important; because a strong part of me had always thought that my parents were right and that if only I had been different, there would not have been trouble in my famly.

Every kid secretly wishes for the death of his parents; when your parents die, you are reborn. By acknowledging these feelings, they lose their power, and you are able to forgive yourself. In the therapeutic experience you confront the things you are most ashamed of, take responsibility for them, and defuse them of their power to destroy your life.

American cities are not built for bitch sessions. Bitch sessions in apartments get neighbors freaked about potential rape or murder. They call the cops, who only find someone screaming at a pillow. What an embarrassment.

I put my father (a big bushy, blue pillow) in the back seat of my car, took my tape recorder, and headed for Golden Gate Park in San Francisco in search of a secluded place to yell my lungs out without embarrassment or restraint.

I found a perfect place, lots of trees, off the main drag. No one in sight. The weather looked a little like rain. It was dark. All the way over in the car I called up scenes from my childhood and shouted, "I hate you, Daddy! Goddamn you! I hate you!" I turned on my tape recorder, grabbed a stick and beat a tree, screaming obscenities at my father. After about ten minutes I heard someone approaching me from behind, and I turned around.

"What are you doing?" he asked.

"I'm having a primal against my father," I said.

"Oh," he said. "I was worried that you were going to damage the tree."

After bitching at my parents in group session, I went to the bathroom, drank two cups of salt water, ate a chocolate cupcake, and stuck two fingers down my throat to vomit the salt and brown shit—vomit them out of my system once and for all!

I could not vomit, I could not let go.

I tried again but to no avail. I wanted to fake it and leave, but something held me back. Mike, a therapist, physically blocked me from going and unmercifully ridiculed me, bringing me close to tears.

"What's wrong, Rubin, you coward, so brave, running around the country overthrowing the government and you can't vomit? Afraid to vomit?" he yelled. "Your sissy mother stopping you from vomiting? You're going to stay here until you vomit, until you get that bitch woman out of your system once and for all!"

I leaned over the toilet, and thrust two fingers down my throat, but just as I was about to gag, I pulled my fingers out. I was scared.

Four therapists gathered around me as I bent over the urinal. They were yelling at me, refusing to let me play my childish "I'm weak" and "I can't do it" games. They loved me too much to let me get away with this phony act. Even as I hated them for their brutal attack, I felt them caring for me. Still I couldn't vomit.

"Jerry, how do you feel?" asked Mike. I felt sick to my stomach with salt water.

"Sick to your stomach! Are you going to stay sick to

your stomach rather than vomit that shit out? That is what you have been doing all your life, hurting your body because you will not get all your parents' bullshit out of you. You'll sacrifice the health of your body for your fears! What an asshole you are!"

Mike said, "Jerry, close your eyes and bring in your guide. Ask your guide why you can't vomit."

I asked Lorraine. At first my child butted in and tried to manipulate her. My child wanted Lorraine to say that I did not have to vomit if I did not want to, that I could do it another time.

But the voice of Lorraine lives deep in the pit of my gut. Lorraine does not lie.

"You can't vomit because you don't *want* to vomit," she said.

The truth of that shook me. I don't want to vomit! I can if I want to, but I do not want to. I am holding onto my parents; I am rebelling against myself.

I relaxed, and right away the white salty shit in the form of my parents' anxiety, fear, and self-hate poured out. I vomited again, and again.

I had so much shit in me that I vomited five times. Each time I felt better, now that I was releasing myself from the psychological poison of my parents. I vomited again. And again! I was happy! I felt free!

And then I ran all the way to Telegraph Avenue in Berkeley, where I treated my child to a chocolate ice cream cone with sprinkles on it.

"With understanding there is no condemnation."
—BOB HOFFMAN

We settle into our seats and close our eyes. What a zap when the group leader asks us to see our mother

147

and father as little children. I had never before thought of my parents as little children.

"As long as you are still angry at your parents, you cannot feel love for them," Dick Russell said. "If you stay angry at your mother, you'll be angry at women all your life."

If I am my mother, then being angry at her means that I am angry at the woman-in-me. I impose the anger at my mother onto my feelings toward other women in my life.

Lorraine said, "Jerry, why continue to hate? If you hate, you carry that hate around with you. It doesn't hurt your father—it hurts only you. Hate is as strong a bond between people as love. As long as you hate your father, you will be tied to him. If you understand your father's childhood, you might learn what made you what you are, and through understanding, free yourself of the patterns you adopted from your father, and from the hypnotic hold your father still has over you. If you put yourself in your father's body, you won't feel anger at him."

I cried for my father at his funeral:

He lies in a blue coffin. My brother is sobbing deeply at the loss of his second parent in two years. This poor man, whose joys were sandwiched between so much grief, spoiled dreams, and unhappiness. We arrive at the cemetery and the coffin is lowered into the ground. I stand over and watch. Inside the coffin I see my father, looking strangely peaceful and beautiful in death.

Inside my father is a little boy, who liked to play sports and run in the streets, and never grew up because he was never loved. A boy who cried all his life for the mommy who never loved him. A boy who wanted so much and got so little.

A cute boy, a sad boy. A boy who loved to eat hot dogs at the ball game. An angry boy, who screamed and yelled to get his way. A boy lived inside my father's body and ran his life. I cried as I saw that boy who never grew up being lowered into the grave.

My father was a dynamic, driving, powerful man with an insatiable hunger and curiosity for life. He was an activist. I picked up his strength, power, and activism. He felt that he could do anything; I have the same optimism.

One day in 1954 while driving his bread truck, he saw a car burst into flames. He leaped from his truck and pulled out a man trapped in the fire. He smothered the fire with his own body, risking his life to save a man he didn't even know.

My father loved to fix things, to do physical labor. I absorbed my father's love of working people and have devoted my life to his causes, although I could never see myself driving a bread truck. Most of my friends are intellectuals, writers, artists, and students. One of the ways I rebelled against my father was by shunning physical labor; at the same time, I developed a political ideology solidly based on support for the working class.

I see myself as a little boy. I see my mother as a little girl. The little boy and the little girl look at each other. The little boy wants to know what happened to the little girl-as-a-child to program her to program me.

I create my mother's defense out of my own imagination. I climb inside her. I become her as a child. I breathe and smell inside her skin. I live in her body. I am her. I write out a conversation between the two children until I cry genuine tears for my mother.

> LITTLE JERRY: Hi, you must be Esther, the little girl who grew up to be my mother. Tell me about your childhood. What made you so out of touch with your body? You taught me to hate my body and live in my head.
>
> LITTLE ESTHER: My father and mother never touched each other. I saw from their example that it was a sin for a man and woman to touch. My mother never held me. Once when I touched my breasts, my father slapped my hand. My mother told me that God punished people who took advantage of their body. I felt my body get cold and freeze because of this lack of touch.
>
> LITTLE JERRY: Do I hate myself as a man because I picked up your dislike of men?
>
> LITTLE ESTHER: Father never listened to me when I spoke, although he treated me as his pet. He never listened to my mother either; he would walk out of the room while she was speaking. My four brothers were jealous of me. I grew up in a family of men where the brothers fought among each other for my father's attention, and resented me because I got it so easily. They felt unloved. One day my brother yelled at me for no reason after a fight he had with Daddy. I ran into my room crying, I was eight years old, I didn't know what I had

done wrong. I blamed myself for the anger my brothers showed me. My father told me that my role in life was to marry a successful man someday.

LITTLE JERRY: You were taught that you were not adequate, that you needed a man to complete you?

LITTLE ESTHER: Yes.

LITTLE JERRY: Maybe that's why I do not feel complete but am looking outside myself for a woman to complete me.

LITTLE ESTHER: Yes, and I got that incompleteness from my mother, who never felt sufficient. I hated men while believing that I needed a man to be whole. I was in terrible pain as a child.

LITTLE JERRY: Mother, I am a victim of male chauvinism! You were treated like shit by men, and you passed *their* shit on to me. Goddamn it! Your childhood was one big hell. You had a terrible time. Compared to you, I am very lucky. You didn't have much of a chance in life, Mother. I just can't hate you anymore.

My throat tightened and my facial muscles stiffened, but I could not cry. Dick asked me to close my eyes and imagine my mother experiencing a brutal death. I still couldn't cry. Dick suggested that I close my eyes and ask Lorraine why I couldn't cry for the unloved child of my mother.

JERRY: Why can't I cry?

LORRAINE: You think it is unmasculine to cry.

Jerry Rubin

JERRY: What can I do?

LORRAINE: Stop *trying* so hard. Relax. Be yourself. Allow the tears—don't force them. You are picking up your parents' prohibition against crying, and their way of covering up their feelings. You hurt so much inside that you have built walls of defenses against your real feelings. If you don't allow yourself to feel bad, you won't allow yourself to feel good.

JERRY: What should I do?

LORRAINE: Repeat over and over again to yourself, "It is O.K. for me to feel, O.K. for a man to cry." See your mother as a little girl, dominated by her father, ignored by her brothers, driven to anxiety by her mother, that poor little girl—what a lonely and sad existence she had! Become her, feel her, put yourself in her body. Relax and let whatever happens happen.

Dick took me through my past. I lay relaxed on the floor and looked into his hypnotic eyes. I completely relaxed all parts of my body as he counted six-five-four-three . . .

Dick had me picture scene after scene in my childhood: scenes of eating, playing, fighting. The scenes went by one by one through my consciousness like a movie. I began to feel what it was like to be back there —my restlessness and nervousness as a child. I felt my father's brusqueness, speed, power, temper; my mother's vulnerability and sadness. I began to feel a little choked up as I kept imagining scenes and then letting them go.

I settled on a scene in our car parked outside the

house I lived in with my parents, grandparents, and Gil. I was in the back seat of the car, my mother was in the front seat, and my father was just getting in the driver's seat. I had just provoked a screaming fight which made my mother feel shitty, and my father was angry. To my mother, I felt, "I'm sorry, Mother," and to my father, "Please don't punish me, Daddy." I felt my hands go up to protect my face against my angry father.

Then I looked at my mother and I felt very sad. I have given this woman a very rough time. Sure, she laid a lot of shit on me, but, as I discovered in our imaginary dialogue, all that shit had been laid on her by her parents and she had had a miserable, lonely, anxious childhood. All she had wanted out of life was love, all she received was loneliness and isolation.

Tears welled up. "Say something to this woman, say what you wanted to say and could not say, Jerry," Dick said. I started to cry and reached out to hold my mother. "I'm sorry, Mother, I didn't mean to hurt you. I'm sorry." I kept picturing my poor mother sitting in the front seat of the car looking so forlorn. Then I flashed to my mother as a young child and that bright, cute, pretty face—also looking scared. My mother as a middle-aged woman and then as a young girl: the two images flashed back and forth, and I felt very, very sad. I began crying and then I held her close and put my arms lovingly around her waist.

Then I saw my mother dying of cancer in the hospital, that poor woman who never lived a loved life. I saw her take her last breath, I saw life leave her cancer-eaten body. And then I remembered her funeral. I saw my cousin Belle overwhelmed with grief at my

153

mother's early death, and all the uncles and aunts, and the rabbi speaking in Hebrew, and poor Gil not knowing what would become of him, and my poor beaten father—alone in the world; doing his best to hold back tears and keep a stiff upper lip; his life shattered; his companion gone. He was later to tell me, "I have nothing left to live for in life—nothing but Gil."

We all passed by the casket to take our last look at the remains of my mother. Then the funeral procession and the long drive to the cemetery. And there I am standing at my mother's grave and watching her being lowered into the ground. And I see inside her, my mother as a little child crying for the love she never got. She cries and cries—my mother's little child is crying—and I stand at the grave, crying, and I say, "I forgive you Mother, I am so sorry about what happened to you in your life. I am sorry how I treated you, I am sorry I was so selfish, I forgive you, Mommy, I am sorry, I forgive you."

I learned sensitivity and gentleness from you, Mother. As an oppressed woman unaware consciously of your oppression, you developed a concern for others which expressed itself in warmth, consideration, and an ability to listen to people. I took that energy from you and expanded it to include blacks, Vietnamese, and other oppressed peoples. I learned from you that compassion, and the positive beauty of shyness. I also learned to develop my intellect. You put me in touch with my spiritual side, my higher self.

You were a strong, valiant woman, fighting the ignorance of the people closest to you, men not even aware of the concept of "sexism." You adapted your-self to the world around you with understanding, toler-ance, and acceptance. The positive side of your sur-render was a calmness and mellowness. I am able now to see and accept your positive, sensitive, giving na-ture.

I am a male victim of male chauvinism. As a child I was taught I needed a woman to survive. If my mother did not love me, I was worthless. So all my life I have longed for the love of a woman—Mother. But at the same time my mother hated herself and her role, and taught me to feel contempt for the very woman whose love I needed for my survival.

Who put my mother in such a position of self-hate? Her father! Her four brothers! Men programmed my mother to hate herself and pass that self-hate on to me. Men, then, are the final victims of male chauvin-ism, a strange twist of karmic fate. Had my mother come in contact with a feminist consciousness, she would have built her internal power independent of men, and passed that self-love on to the men in her life.

Then Dick had me flash to Ruthie and Rhoda. I see Ruthie crying. I see Rhoda as a little girl crying out for love, to be held, cared for. I see an endless stream of fights, losses of temper, and breakdowns in com-munication. And then I flash to this realization: I do not see Ruthie or Rhoda. I see only the woman I need to make me complete. I use and need Rhoda for my benefit, and I am losing her because I do not answer to her needs. I am too busy trying to get her to fulfill mine. What a tearful, sad realization: I have never

155

loved in my life. I do not know how to love. I *need* too much to be able to love. I never saw my mother, I never saw Ruthie or Rhoda.

Tears pour down my face as I picture my mother, Ruthie, Rhoda. For the first time in my life I have seen these three women as they are, not as I need or want them to be. I forget myself and I see them, and my whole body cries.

For that brief instant I feel what love is. *Love is seeing the other person.* Love is giving for the pure unselfish act of giving. I want to start seeing people as they are and not as extensions of myself. I want to stop using people and start loving them—or I will die. I can give only by seeing people as they are, not as my needs make them out to be. I want to love!

Chapter 12

Learning to Forgive Myself

I WAS on my way to a tantric yoga workshop when the telephone rang. Dick had a bombshell to lay on me. He had noticed in reading my emotional biography that for six years as a child I had lived upstairs in the house with my mother's parents, my grandmother and grandfather. "These two people, your grandmother and grandfather, had a powerful effect on you, Jerry," Dick said. "I want you to begin processing them immediately."

I cancelled my workshop and went to work. My brains

were blown by what I discovered while listing my grandparents' negative traits, prosecuting and then defending and forgiving them. Those two ancient people —my grandmother and grandfather—I was just like them!

Not only did I discover that I *am* my grandmother and grandfather, but I began to see that in my blood are the values and beliefs of nineteenth-century Russia! Here I am—a modern, hip, radical yippie. But if you look close, what I really am is a nineteenth-century Russian orthodox religious Jew. That is my programming. My grandmother and grandfather not only programmed my mother directly, they got me during the formative years I spent with them.

As I listed my grandmother's traits and beliefs, I was embarrassed to discover that on a deep, unconscious level I had copied her act. My grandmother educated me to be a sex-starved male chauvinist! I remember, when I was five years old, playing with myself in bed, enjoying the total sensuality of getting in touch with my body. My grandmother entered the room and screamed: "Get your hands away from that! Don't touch yourself like that!" I froze and pulled my hands away from my cock.

My family goes to the synagogue. Grandma goes upstairs to join the women, who are segregated from the men. The women sit quietly upstairs, observing the men downstairs who are solemnly listening to the prayers as the sacred Torah is revealed. Even though I am only seven, I am allowed to join my grandfather and father downstairs. During the break I go upstairs to visit with Grandma. She is not permitted to come to the men's section because she is a woman—passive, second-class, only a spectator by the rules of the religion, which she deeply believes in. She believes in her own inferiority.

I remember during yippie meetings the "men" talked their business and humored the women when they began to talk, not expecting to hear anything "worthwhile." During all that time I was seeing, not Joan, Barbara, or Laurie, but my grandma on the second floor of the synagogue watching my grandfather with the men downstairs.

My grandmother had a far-out sense of humor and must be included along with Lenny Bruce among the inspirations for yippie. She raised four sons who became comics, one a vaudeville performer; their humor was a charming humanism—except when it edged into hostility disguised as satire. The humor I got from my grandmother addresses itself to the human condition, especially its suffering. The sense of the absurd which contributed to yippie was channeled from my grandmother.

The detective story of my life becomes even more intriguing when I consider that I was programmed by people I never saw. My grandmother's parents programmed my grandmother to program me. That ties the living origins of my programming back to the eighteenth century!

I had a hard time bitching against my grandfather. My grandfather loved me, and favored me over all his other grandchildren. He put me on his knee and told me story after story, and drove me around in his car as if he were my chauffeur. He was the best grandfather a boy ever had. How could I be angry at such a dear old man?

159

But my grandfather in the guise of love was really programming me to be just like him: to believe that my race and religion were superior to all others; to fear and distrust a paranoid world that murdered Jews. He gave me my buttons of racism, paranoia, and fear.

In favoring me above his other grandchildren, my grandfather taught me to win self-esteem by feeling superior to others. My grandfather continually told me, "Jerry, I like you so much better than Johnny." It felt good. Grandfather was giving me an ego massage. But he was also driving me to spend the next thirty years looking for "Johnnys" to be better than in order to please the grandfather-inside-me.

I learned devotion and intensity from my grandfather. He gave me my first political education, explaining the difference between those who work for a living and those who own. When I was a kid I hated my grandfather spending hours in the synagogue doing nothing but saying the same prayer all day, over and over again, shaking his body back and forth.

Now I see my grandfather as a high Zen monk emptying his mind by repeating the same mantra. He meditated four to six hours a day, although he didn't call it "meditating." While praying to "God," he was really getting high, losing his ego, dancing in cosmic consciousness. I extended my rebellion against my grandfather to a distaste for all rituals and religious activity, even meditation. Repeating a chant reminds me too much of my grandfather in religious prayer. Now that I see my grandfather as a man living in a totalitarian world of one consciousness, I can appreciate his getting high through religion and not allow that path to be blocked for me. I carried my grand-father's faith and intensity with me into my political activity of the 1960's.

When my parents died, I felt responsible for my thirteen-year-old brother, Gil, and I became his sur-rogate parent and legal guardian. I was an even worse parent than my mother and father! I repeated the cardinal parental sin, "I know what's best for you." It was my "responsibility" to direct his life. He would understand when he grew up that I did it all for his own good.

I was "sacrificing" myself for him. Why didn't he appreciate all that I was giving up for him? I set real standards for him; I wanted my "son" to be the best! I had to protect him as much as possible. If I let him alone, he might turn out to be a Hare Krishna singer or a Jesus Freak.

I was forced to punish Gil and even hit him to get him to respect me. My father used to whip me with a strap to get me to "respect" him, and here I was doing the same thing to my kid brother. I had rebelled against my parents, but in truth I had become a carbon-copy parent.

Before psychic therapy I had a hard time admitting that I was oppressive as a parent. Seeing what my parents did to me liberated me to see what I did to Gil. Please forgive me, Gil, I didn't understand what I was doing.

My brother and I have become very close. We had difficulty as children because I played the role of "bad boy" and Gil was the "good boy." Gil took up my mother's interest in piano and practiced six hours a day, becoming an accomplished classical pianist and appearing as a featured performer in concerts. He graduated from college with a degree in music, then decided he wanted to become a doctor and studied pre-med courses in chemistry and biology for two years. He eventually decided on dental school and is now studying at the Columbia School of Dentistry.

When we are together, even though I am nine years older, people look at us and think he is the older one. People don't believe we are brothers—we don't look alike, yet on a psychic level the similarities begin. Both of us have the same barriers in expressing intimacy on a deep level. We share an ability to work in a disciplined, almost obsessive-compulsive manner. On the outer level, I look like and act like our father; Gil takes after our mother. Inwardly we both absorbed both of them.

I have come to some powerful realizations: I am not so different after all from the mother I have been trying to avoid all my life, the father I seem so different from, the grandmother and grandfather that seem so foreign to my modern ways. The more I rebelled against them, the more I became like them. In fact, I *am* my mother and father! I *am* my grandparents! If I hate them, I hate myself.

That realization is like an acid rush, at once terrifying and completely liberating.

"I don't have to hide anymore!"

"I am what I am!"

"I am my mother! I am my father!"

I am standing on the shoulders of my parents and grandparents in our cooperative venture through the karma of life. They are in me, and in loving myself I love them.

Suddenly the living spirits of the most important people in my life appear before me in my imagination. To my left are my mother and grandmother, behind them their parents, and behind them their parents. To my right are my father and grandfather, and behind them their parents, and behind them their parents. Also present are my brother, lovers, ex-lovers, and friends.

Tears are flowing down the faces of my parents and friends. They feel the love that I have for them. The God in me loves the God in them; the child in me loves the child in each of them. They forgive me for what I did in the past. I forgive them.

A month later, I had a stomach ache for two days. My negative programming was telling me that I had an ulcer. My stomach said, "Stop sending so much ice cream, sweets, and sugar down here." My stomach was actually preparing me for a major change.

Then, driving across the Golden Gate Bridge, I had the sneaky feeling that Lorraine was leaving me. Still embarrassed about talking to spirits, I asked her, but instead of Lorraine I saw a thin, white man in his early forties, with a narrow face and brown hair, jumping around like crazy in white shorts. I noticed his tight, taut, muscled body. "Tony" kept exercising. I tried to talk with him but he didn't seem very verbal. He communicated a feeling that Lorraine had left because her warmth was no longer needed, and from now on I needed a disciplinarian inside me to help me get myself together. Tony jumps up and down with the message, "Let's get down to business!" His very body speaks one word: "DISCIPLINE."

"If you were not ready for me, you would not have

called me to come," said Tony. "It is amazing, Jerry, how hard it is for you to see what is right under your nose. I am here to help you see the obvious. That means living in paradox, to be master of your ship and at the same time a leaf in the wind, to direct yourself and let yourself be directed, to move with decision and flow."

Tony and I have had a strange relationship. He drives me into situations without telling me first. A year later, I began the forty-day Arica training. In the middle of a meditation I saw Tony's body jumping around. He lured me into Arica without telling me. Tony's presence tells me that it is not enough to plan —I must do. Tony does. I got the spirit guide—the internal guru—that I need.

Chapter 13

est

WERNER ERHARD stood in the front of the room and shouted at us, "You spend your entire life trying to cover up the fact that you are assholes!" He was attacking the personality we present to the world, our "acts." I sat in est and held on to my act, furious at Werner for raking in money by calling us names. Where would he have been in mid-1960's when the United States was defoliating Vietnam? He would have been calling the protesters "assholes"!

I felt like leaping out of my seat and strangling the

motherfucker, and then making a grand exit. But if I stood up and attacked Werner, two hundred and fifty other people would look at me and say, "There's Jerry Rubin doing his Jerry Rubin number." Werner had me trapped. I'd be damned if I would be the example to prove his point that we go through our lives *playing* ourselves rather than *being* ourselves.

In mere description est (Erhard Seminars Training) sounds absurd. About two hundred people are packed into a hotel room on hard chairs for four eighteen-hour days. Everyone agrees in advance not to eat, leave their seats, or talk unless called on. From the front of the room the trainer barrages people with an attack on their egos, roles, and life-styles, while at the same time giving academic lectures on the nature of reality, the meaning of life, and the process of perception. Then people go to the microphone to share from their hearts and souls the secrets they rarely tell their friends. At the end everyone is enlightened.

Now Werner is teaching me that I control my body; my body does not control me. I am one of fifty thousand people who have been through est. But I sit there feeling like an absolute ass. "Rubin," I think to myself, "you'd fall for anything that promised you the moon."

I figured "Werner Erhard" was a Nazi from Germany. All my Jewish anti-German feelings bubbled to the surface. But Werner is actually a Jew whose real name is Jack Rosenberg, and he's from Philadelphia. He ran away from home at the age of twenty-two and renamed himself after Ludwig Erhard and Werner Von Braun. I decided to leave quietly.

This was another of my acts: to hide or withdraw, the reverse side of my activist act. I play the superior one who looks down on others, the person who can't be conned. I wasn't going to fall for Werner's double talk. I was thinking all these things but was scared to go up to the microphone where, one by one, people were telling their life stories. I worried that I might not have something brilliant to say. What if people thought, "Gee, Jerry Rubin is boring." I'm a great orator when a thousand people are applauding, but in est I'd have to make it on my own. So, instead I sat quietly, putting down all the assholes who went to the microphone to tell their dull inner dramas. Werner was right. These people *were* assholes. I couldn't wait to leave.

Then I remembered: "I paid $200 to sit through this shit! I know what to do! I'll run to the bank early Monday morning and cancel my check. That'll screw Werner's ass!" That night I went home to sleep. The next morning I woke up at 6 A.M. feeling refreshed. My conscious mind had quit est training, but my unconscious mind had other plans for me. I found myself zooming over to the hotel to beat the other assholes to a front-row seat.

Something theatrically revolutionary was happening at est. In the 1960's we had used political guerrilla theater to get people to see beyond their roles. Now Werner was creating a psychological theater provoking people into self-confrontation. Whenever people discover themselves, they grow and learn—and that has to be revolutionary. (My act is liking something *only* if I can call it "revolutionary.")

The key to the 1970's is the consciousness revolution. External events are important in determining consciousness, but in the end we decide exactly *how* to respond to any event that takes place in our lives. The current consciousness changes reflect the growing awareness by people of their own power: "I control my consciousness, my inner reality."

Throughout history only a minority have dropped out of society to reach higher states of consciousness. Today thousands of people are going through spiritual and psychological transformations. Est is spreading throughout the middle class—to professionals, intellectuals, businessmen, housewives, students, right-wingers, left-wingers.

The consciousness movement is a direct descendant of the grass-acid movement of the 1960's. Grass and acid are tools for altering consciousness, but direct control of consciousness through internal discipline is the goal. All the consciousness movements use various forms of psychic healing, returning the responsibility of health to the people.

Back in the est hotel room for the second day, I was lapsing again into a conscious sleep, feeling superior and contemptuous, ripped off and conned, shy and scared. There was nowhere to go, no one to call, no distraction. I was alone with myself—something that seldom occurs in my life since I am usually too busy doing my act. Doing est we could not talk to each other or leave our seats or read or take notes. If someone left his seat, two est staff members sent him back.

My body felt itchy, my mind bored. Werner kept saying that we create everything that happens to us. Had I created my itchy body and bored mind? *How often* is my body itchy and my mind bored?

The people at the microphone telling their personal dramas were about as interesting as afternoon TV soap operas, but I heard my own in everybody else's story. Listening to these straight housewives and button-down businessmen, I realized that I was just like them. Once we got past our acts, our costumes, we all had the same experiences. Suddenly I felt sympathy for Richard Nixon, Nelson Rockefeller, Gerald Ford. Strip away the mask and the role, and there hides a scared human being behind our acts.

As a child I believed that underneath we were all the same. I believed in God. When you died you would relive your life again, but this time experiencing the feelings of everyone who had interacted with you. Heaven was a big movie theater. One day sitting in the library in high school I had a cosmic realization. What if at this very moment I am simultaneously living my life in the body and consciousness of everyone else on the planet?

Later, my political activities were motivated by basic feelings of equality: a Vietnamese peasant is equal to a Wall Street executive. Everything that makes us different from one another is artificial: all human beings basically want and need the same things—security, love, energy.

Unconsciously I had accepted my environment's definition of the differences between human beings: "We are Americans and they are not; we are free and they are Communists; we are Jewish and they are goyim; we are white and they are black; we are good and they are criminals." Then, when I was in jail with a guard who sadistically brutalized the prisoners, I realized that underneath his act and his scared macho personality—he was me and I was him.

Snapping back to the present, I heard Werner

screaming that we create everything that happens to us in our lives. Like a yippie, he took his point to an absurd extreme. He said that Vietnamese babies created the napalm that fell on their heads, that Jews constructed Auschwitz, that rape victims desired to be raped. The audience went crazy, screaming, turning off, throwing up their hands in outrage. Werner ran around the room arguing his theory of self-responsibility with each person, obviously trying to offend, shock, scare, create a mood. He listened to people's miseries —their parents' deaths, broken marriages, financial tragedies—and then laughed in their faces and screamed: "YOU ASSHOLE, YOU CAUSED IT!"

Werner was telling a young woman that she *wanted* to be beaten, raped, robbed. He offered not one iota of sympathy; he certainly is no Jewish Mother. He hears about a tragedy and shrugs his shoulders. "So what!" he says. "So what!"

The room lightened up a bit. People considered what he was saying. Maybe I did create my auto accident. Maybe I did create my cancer. Maybe I did kill my mother. Maybe I'm not a helpless victim. A huge sigh echoed across the room. One woman took the microphone and said, "I had polio as a kid. I see now I wanted polio, I chose my polio." People took a look at the worst thing in their lives, took full responsibility for it, and then realized, "So what?" Nothing makes a difference. Romantic breakups, sickness, death—so what? I caused it all, accepted or resisted it. I created everything that happened to me, even my parents. Do I want to feel sad about it, happy, or what?

"It is up to you!" screams Werner.

I thought of my life, the loneliness, pain, rejection; and I heard Werner's voice inside me shouting at me, "What a big soap opera, you fool! You brought it all on yourself! You wanted it! You plan your colds, your headaches, your insomnia—everything! Now dig it!"

Werner's sheer intensity kept me in the room. He reminded me of Lenny Bruce provoking people. Suddenly I flashed on what Werner was doing. He was a Zen master trying to shock people out of their minds. Werner screams: "Do you get it? Do you get it? The moment you get it, you'll lose it. The truth is an experience, not a belief!"

Next, Werner went to the blackboard and in an abstract lecture tried to convince us that we had never made a *free* choice in our lives. We had chosen all that happened to us, but we were mere robots playing out our childhood programming. More objections!

"Whattaymean! I chose my career! I chose my wife! I chose my philosophy! I chose my personality!"

"No! No!" screamed Werner, "you are all machines, you have never made a decision in your life." This time people started getting "it" quickly. "The truth is an experience, a Zen koan. It makes no sense to the mind," said Werner.

Is there a consciousness beyond my mind? Around the room people's eyes were lighting up as they screamed: "I got it! I got it!" I wanted to get it too. What if everyone got it but me? I'd miss out on my $200, and feel inferior besides. Werner had created a group atmosphere in which everyone now wanted to "get it."

To get it I would have to give up my identity, beliefs; my feelings of being ripped-off, my repulsion at being part of group pressure, my rationality, my logical mind, my individuality; my ego, my role, my name. Me! I'd have to give up control to someone I didn't even trust. I'd have to relinquish my rebel role and all my resistance. Worst of all, I'd have to give up my freedom.

A lot of things exist between me and the world. I am all the things that define and defend me. Sitting there in est I admitted for a second to myself how much I play the "I'm right-you're wrong" game. That was my approach to life. I peeked outside myself and saw my personality, my games, my trip—The Whole Jerry Rubin Show—and it hurt to look.

I saw that I had created every part of the story to the last detail. It hurt to see so clearly, and it scared me. What if I could see myself so clearly all the time? I set up everything in my life to happen just the way it happens. I felt totally free! Totally powerful —and totally scared to death! I would never be able to lie to myself again.

Werner had permanently altered my consciousness. *I am responsible* for everything that happens to me. If I am miserable, I choose to be miserable. It is up to me: To like it or hate it. To choose. To become the center of my life.

Every condition in the body is determined by the nervous system. When we suffer with a headache, for example, we do not experience the headache, but the past pictures in our minds of headaches. Our eagerness to give our condition a conceptual name, like a "headache" or "cold"—with all the memories the word conjures up—strengthens the condition. Our feeling that we are victims and can do nothing gives the condition power over us.

Like a faith healer, Werner brought people with headaches to the front of the room. He had them experience directly the sensations, naming the location, size, shape, and color of the pain. He had them relate those sensations to pictures and emotional experiences in the past. "Do you want those sensations?" Deciding they did not, focusing directly on the sensations, people began losing the headaches, backaches, and nervous conditions that had plagued them for years.

Next Werner attacked the "seekers" of the 1970's, the growth trippers who go from rolfing to bioenergetics to yoga to tai chi to est to natural foods to gestalt to TM to swamis in search of the "answer." I recognized myself. "Goddamnit, Jerry, you're a guru whore," Sam Keen once ribbed me, after hearing I did Arica after psychic therapy after est. In two years in the growth movement I had tried everything, looking, looking, looking. Werner shouted at us: "WHAT THE HELL ARE YOU LOOKING FOR? THIS IS IT! THERE IS NOTHING TO FIND! YOU'VE FOUND IT! THERE IS NOTHING IN LIFE BUT THIS! YOU'RE HERE! YOU'VE ARRIVED! LOOK AND SEE IT!"

The truth jarred me. All my life I've been obsessed with the idea of seeking, searching, working for some mythical tomorrow. Life is a ladder: climb, climb, climb. To get where?

I have had money and I know its emptiness. I've eaten expensive meals and when they are over I'm full. I've experienced good sex—and gotten used to it. I've gone up and come down from LSD. I've felt myself in the center of history and it's passed. I've traveled —and it's all the same place. I've met the very rich and powerful and discovered that it's the same at the bottom as it is at the top.

Jerry Rubin

When I wasn't at the top, I was trying to get there. When I got there I was trying to stay there. In neither place did I experience "there." It was always tomorrow that I worried about. Now I see that there is no tomorrow, only right now.

"THERE IS NOTHING TO FIND! THERE IS NO TOMORROW! TOMORROW IS TODAY! THERE IS NOTHING NOTHING NOTHING! THIS IS IT! And it doesn't matter! When you are dead, you will be dead," said Werner, "and not one second sooner."

This is it? What I have been hoping for, looking for? Nowhere to go but here? People in the room began screaming at the discovery that there is nowhere to go. I could literally feel the tension disappear. I saw faces lighten. My shoulders relaxed and I felt a full feeling in my stomach. Time slowed down. I felt like the richest man on earth. Because I had everything. I had The Moment, my life in my hands.

Est had sent me inside myself. I've spent time feeling sorry for myself because I did not get what I wanted. But inside, a voice beyond my normal consciousness whispered, "Jerry, if you'd pay attention to what actually happened, rather than what you wanted, you'd be happy." In est I was again hearing that intuitive psychic insight. Werner was telling me: "Your mind never knows what's going on. Your mind lives in its own world of self-justifying need. Pay attention to what is actually happening and be there. Stop living in the pictures of your head. You cause pain for yourself with your expectations and preconceptions."

Throughout the activism of the 1960's I aimed for a goal, but never achieved the precise goal in my mind. As long as I kept my attention on the goal, I always felt disappointed. But if I paid attention to the process, to what *actually happened to me*, then I could never be dissatisfied!

In the 1960's we were demonstrating and holding meetings to make political changes tomorrow. But through it all a psychic part of me knew the truth: We were demonstrating and meeting not for tomorrow, but for today. We were doing what we were doing for the doing of it. While doing, we were *being* our doing.

I saw that I had a scarcity approach to life—there is not enough, I better get mine! "Stop looking for what you've already got," said Werner. The room at that point was high as a balloon. Everybody was digging the moment. We were out of our minds.

But my mind kept fighting back. "Will living in the moment destroy my desire to create and change?" My behavior will not necessarily change but my *awareness* will change. Instead of seeking with the expectation of finding, I experience my seeking as an end in itself. I become one with my seeking, and merge with the moment.

I kept getting this insight, then losing it. It wouldn't stick. I don't experience life because I keep wanting life to come out a certain way. If I keep it up, I'll be laying on my death bed and wondering what happened. Where'd my life go?

But living totally in the moment is scary. It goes against years of conditioning. Still, it works. When I put my awareness completely in what I am doing, I make whatever I do work.

"You can't change anything by complaining about it," said Werner, "so why complain? You change something when you change it, not one second before. And if you complain about it, experience yourself complaining about it. Enjoy your complaining!"

Even though I make decisions every day, on the deepest level I don't have a damn thing to do with my life. I flow with events and do not consciously know what is going on. I have to accept this confusion, because I cannot be in control. I can take responsibility for what happens, but in the end self-responsibility is an illusion too.

As soon as I learn to give up and stop trying to understand-control-plan-direct everything, I feel in tune with the energy of life. "I don't know" turns out to be three high words.

Werner Erhard is taking the mystery out of the spiritual experience. The spiritual movement has always been represented by swamis speaking foreign languages, meditation with strange-sounding foreign mantras, and uncomfortable yoga positions. Spirituality has been for the select few, techniques passed down by word-of-mouth, deliberately kept from the masses. Est is an attempt to Americanize Eastern consciousness—to make it available to the majority of people.

In an instant I flashed on the truth. Everything is process. The spiritual movement of the 1970's, from Zen to Don Juan, is driving home the same point: *see* the moment. Werner said by experiencing the moment *as it is,* I automatically receive pleasure from it, therefore automatically experience my life changing for the better.

In a time when people feel powerless to change society, est is teaching people they can control their own lives. As the New Consciousness movement's answer to Billy Graham, Werner is teaching human beings that they are powerful. Est has exploded the psychological hydrogen bomb: awareness. Control awareness and you control yourself. Change awareness and you change yourself.

In putting together est, Werner has borrowed from yoga, Gurdjieff, Carlos Castaneda, Fritz Perls, self-hypnosis, scientology, transactional analysis, John Lilly, and you name it in the consciousness area. Everyone sees his thing in est—it's gestalt, it's Zen, it's yippie. Werner has taken the truth from esoteric ideas and philosophies, and is serving it up like chicken soup for the masses, in a chain of consciousness supermarkets which are subversively transforming consciousness.

Werner has been called the Eddie Fisher of Zen, and the Hugh Hefner of higher consciousness. Est devotees think that he is a being from another planet in a human body. Werner has created an army of little Werners: followers with plastic smiles, name tags, and a mindless use of est rhetoric. They are trying to hold on to an experience, forgetting that Werner said, "You can't hold on to enlightenment. It comes and goes." The moment you try and hold on, you go off.

Est is a mass of contradictions. It teaches spontaneity and realness, but produces people with a sorority-fraternity superficiality. It preaches individuality, yet est graduates end up looking, talking, and acting alike. The training is rebellious, provoking, outrageous, yet in society est itself respects position and authority and spends time trying to get accepted by the traditional power centers.

Est preaches self-responsibility, yet it barrages people by mail, telephone, and in person to continue with est in seminars and follow-up programs. Est preaches living in the moment, yet its organization works on a strict definition of time. It preaches power to the people, yet all real power is held by Werner. Est claims to be in the center of energy, yet it makes no comment on anything political in our society. Est people say to live in your body, but in practice they live in their heads, coming off very asexual.

Est preaches honesty, yet all salaries are secret. If you think est is a fascist corporation, an est staff member will tell you, as one told me, "You must examine your pictures of fascist corporations to see what we are reactivating."

Everyone's job in est is to re-create Werner. Judy, the telephone operator, takes responsibility for re-creating Werner. By doing exactly what Werner wants, she takes responsibility for it and accepts her servitude as freedom. As Werner puts it, taking responsibility for my lack of freedom, I become free. Judy thinks that she is a free being even though she answers the est phone, "Hello, est, this is Judy, how may I assist you?" knowing that she has no power to be spontaneous and real.

Est ideology prevents them from seeing the lack of freedom in their situation. They have turned Zen into an organizational justification, and destroyed Zen aliveness in the process.

I was once stopped at the door and prevented from entering an est function by an est person. I accused him of following orders without thinking. He told me that he had chosen to follow orders, and that therefore it was a free choice. He was cleverly using Zen to justify authoritarianism.

Est people do a funny thing with attachment. They justify their attachment by saying, "I'm really unattached but I have chosen." What is the objective difference between attached attachment and unattached attachment? In the latter you can give it up. But what if you never give it up?

Werner told me that he feels no identification with his name, his status, his ego, his power. He has purged himself of all ego and all desire, and is experiencing life directly. If Werner changed his name back to Jack Rosenberg, he would be demonstrating to est addicts what nonattachment really means, with the example of his own life. He would be making a political statement.

Est's eventual death is contained within its life. It is building a top-down organization with a huge staff and yearly budget in the millions. The nature of the est corporate structure may make it move in a conservative direction. Est people are applying the latest theories in motivational research and capitalistic business efficiency. Material needs may triumph over spiritual concerns.

Werner means it when he says that human beings basically are machines. Find out how they work and you can control them easily. He gives people no responsibility and then cons them into believing that they have total responsibility—all the while telling them that they are beyond beliefs!

Werner himself may not be aware of all this. He is naive politically, and believes the way to solve problems is top-down and corporate. He implicitly trusts the American business solution to problems: he even hired a former vice-president of Coca-Cola to preside over est. When the est organization corrupts itself, Werner may be as surprised as other people.

Jerry Rubin

Werner incorporates into est the American ideology of each-person-for-himself, preaching a modern-day Horatio Algerism. He does not stress collective social change. Est gives the old American "make it" philosophy a new Eastern Zen twist. What is needed is an internal revolution within est to replace its "You can be powerful and make it in our society" aspect with the Zen "Freedom is giving it all up." Then, Werner might replace his stress on individual power with an equal stress on collective love and power.

I have a feeling that history may be using Werner Erhard. He is not aware of the subversive influence that Zen will have on the American psyche. Stronger than marijuana, Zen will weaken the will of people to compete, achieve, dominate. The ethic of competition, achievement, and domination is the core of the American system. Est may contribute to a spiritual alternative to Christianity. As a high man turning people on to their natural rhythms, Werner may not realize the full political impact of what he is doing in transforming human beings.

At times I wanted to be an est trainer, envying the mind-bending power of changing people. But to become an est trainer I would have to become a total likeness of Werner. I'd have to choose my lack of freedom, and become free. Even though est is organized like a capitalist corporation, it justifies itself in quasi-religious, elitist terms like a Communist party with Werner at the top. Werner as a symbol is to est what Mao as a symbol is to China: a myth of truth and authority, an example, a unifier.

Despite all these criticisms, I encourage my friends to take est. It is a powerful emotional house-cleaning, a personal experience in self-knowledge. For a few weeks after est I felt as high as I've ever felt in my life. If somebody sneered at me, I had created the sneer. If I woke up feeling low, I had created my lowness. I went around making miracles, creating everything that was happening to me.

How strong we could be if we controlled our consciousness, our acts, our body processes! What a massive exercise in mass education Werner has created: a school, church, theater, mass ritual, spiritual movement, humanistic psychology's answer to the Jesus Freaks.

As a result of est, I am more conscious of my awareness than I have ever been in my life. I am not attached to my awareness of the moment; I see how I deliberately can select positive or negative awareness. I pay a lot of attention to how my expectations bring on results. When something "bad" happens, I ask myself: Did I bring it about with my expectation? Did I psychically create it?

Taking est I was able to break for a moment my identification with the things that run my life. I expanded my awareness to see how mechanical is my behavior. Changing is another question. That takes practice and discipline.

Est will spread like wildfire throughout America. It addresses itself to basic human needs, and does work by giving people a greater sense of themselves. In many ways it was the most powerful growth experience I had. But when it was over I realized that neither est nor yoga nor biofeedback can do it for me. The experience recedes into memory, the techniques fade. And I am left with only one resource—me.

Chapter 14

Waiting for Life's Pure Moments

AFTER est and psychic therapy, I did the forty-day Arica training, an experience combining physical work on the body with meditation. The Arica theory is that spirituality means nothing unless expressed physically in the body. As long as energy exists in the mind, it is not in the body. All Arican exercises are geared to bringing energy from the head into the kath, a place four inches below the navel, the midpoint of the body and the key place for the Eastern martial arts. A person with consciousness in his kath is in control of himself.

The Arica eight-hour-a-day training set out to transform my body biochemistry. For forty days I went without sweets, meat, starch, and carbohydrates to clean out my system. We did the "Arica gym" every morning, an intensive system of yoga-like exercises combining movement with conscious breathing. We spent other hours in various forms of meditation, concentrating on colors, sounds, or group chanting. Arica is a hedonistic spiritual trip, rooted in the body, in physical movement, in control of one's energy balance.

The Arica exercises were culled from many disciplines. The program was put together by Oscar Ichazo, the son of a Bolivian general, whose background reveals his respect for authority, discipline, and order. In the early 1970's he invited Americans to come study with him in the town of Arica, Chile. He eventually moved to New York, and Arica now has spread to thirty cities.

My mind always found something to think about when I meditated or held awkward body positions. I felt how the chattering of my mind—which Arica says is 99 per cent unnecessary—dominated my attention. By cutting down on mental chatter, I learn to observe myself directly and objectively.

Arica uses various techniques to practice centering consciousness physically in the kath. We took walks through the city repeating a sound in our heads, experiencing everything we saw directly, without concepts. So much of my life I have spent seeing concepts rather than sensations. Now, by repeating a sound over and over, I jammed my mental airwaves, shutting off my constant internal chatter.

As the climax of the training, "the desert," I spent

forty-eight hours alone, without music, reading or writing materials, or a telephone. The goal is sensory deprivation in order to practice self-observation, to observe myself doing what I do without judgment. If I throw a panic, observe myself: "Look, I'm throwing a panic."

I ended up in a huge house in Staten Island and went through the forty-eight hours, learning about myself. I watched myself masturbate six times, give myself two nightmares, almost go crazy with fear and panic once, and think the desert was over when I had twelve hours left.

I made a breakthrough. I met my panic and lived through it. I experienced the fear that I could not go to sleep without having nightmares as I lay in bed with nothing to do or read, tossing and turning. The aloneness freaked me. I looked at myself and realized in my gut that I was giving myself fear.

There was nothing to be afraid of. My fear was a decision, a choice. I could experience the fear and demystify it. I dropped the fear and fell asleep. I think that what I actually feared was my own death. After the desert I felt more rooted in my stomach. I watched me look at me, my body, my personality and say, "This is me!"

Arica exercises train people to see, feel, and experience without thoughts. Like est, Arica makes a total assault on beliefs. In the political days of the sixties I would never have put up with this attitude toward beliefs. I was a believer: I believed in revolution, the movement, socialism. I was attached to my beliefs. I saw any attack on my belief structure as a reactionary attack on my beliefs.

Doing est and Arica, I looked at the very process of believing. Beliefs set preconditions and determine perceptions. Most of my beliefs are totally arbitrary and unconscious. Living without beliefs is impossible, and I still have them, but I am less attached to them now.

Seeing the beliefs that create my negative feelings makes me feel better. It is *my* beliefs, not outside incidents, which cause my suffering. I try to see life exactly as a movie camera would see, without feelings, interpretations, or expectations, but as neutral actions. All the spiritual disciplines maintain that nobody can hurt me but myself. Whenever somebody else "hurts" me, it is because my mind believes it and tells my body. So much of the pain in my life is mental—me doing it to me!

Arica is a trip without words. Teachers refuse to give any information on what to expect. They teach by getting their personalities out of the way, embodying themselves as clear channels passing on techniques from Oscar. As a result, they seem at times like robots. Their goal is to rid themselves of personality, which they say is an expression of ego. The men wear short hair and are clean-shaven; the women are lean and lithe.

I fidgeted my way through the entire Arica training, receiving the award for the fidgiest meditator Arica ever had. By the last day I was deliberately sticking my feet in the middle of the circle in open rebellion against the serious "religious" rituals.

Even if I didn't become a total Arican, and didn't reach a state of thoughtless meditation, I had taken a step. What progress I made is progress. I have slowed down, put my body on a healthy regimen, learned to control my mind, learned specific techniques for relaxing my body and mellowing out my emotions.

Aricans discipline their energy: they are spiritual Spartans. During the training I'd hang out with non-spiritual friends who were drinking and eating rich foods, running through exciting New York gossip, ego-oriented success-motivated conversations. In New York, as Phil Ochs said, people talk about their careers or diseases. My mental machinery was telling me things like: I am better than these people because I am working on losing my ego! I am spiritually superior! But spiritual superiority is another form of ego.

To Arica *all* ego satisfactions are empty and ultimately defeats. An ego death is necessary for true happiness. Some people give it all up and get absorbed in Arica; most use Arica techniques to create a healthy ego.

I never want to lose my aggressiveness or my ego completely, nor my tense energy. As an activist I catalyzed other people; my role in the movement was enthusiast, promoter, motivator. I do not want to help create a society in which meditation totally eliminates rebellion. I want to add meditation to my life, but thank God for politics and action!

As I grow older, I am going back to my childhood feelings about God. God is the highest state of consciousness, total awareness of everything at all times. My goal in life is to get as close as I can to God, to a total awareness, and to act on that awareness. The more aware and conscious I become, the more I am ready to accept my death.

For the first time in my life I believe in the non-physical realm, a plane of existence which we cannot perceive with our senses, but which exists beyond our normal consciousness. Specific training in meditation and internal discipline can help us harness that energy to aid our lives on the planet. I think that physical death is a beginning as well as an ending. I have no proof of this. It's a feeling—and faith.

Reincarnation is helping us accept our deaths. I want to die, not fighting death, but in my usual excited way, looking forward to where I am going! I'm not in a hurry, yet when I die I want to enjoy the process of dying as another adventure in living.

I look differently now at the deaths of my parents. I believe that my dead parents are still alive as spirits. I am turning negative memories into positive learning experiences. The spirits of my parents appreciate this use of their earthplane karma. I love them and I know I will meet their spirits again.

The "observer" role is the key to every growth trip I have done, the answer to neurosis, the political dynamite of the growth movement. By learning how to look objectively at ourselves, we free ourselves from limitations to growth.

As I look at my life, I see it has often been one series of big illusions, self-seductions. My dream is never the reality I experience. But the dream gives me the energy to go on. Depression for me is when I have no illusion or dreams to inspire me. Illusion is my alcohol, my speed, my form of escape.

Oh, such illusions! Cuba the revolutionary state! Israel the homeland! Guerrilla revolutionary war in America! The Perfect Couple! Yippie! Grass! Socialism! Acid! est! Psychic Therapy! Ruthie, Rhoda, the women in my life! Illusion after illusion!

Jerry Rubin

At the age of thirty-seven I have seen many of my dreams go up in smoke. One alternative is cynicism: life is one big disappointment, not even worth dreaming about. Cynicism is a protection against disappointment—an emotional scab that protects against feeling more pain. But cynicism is an illusion too. All is illusion. The most important thing for me is to choose positive illusions.

I have my Pure Moments, moments of universal oneness and universal nowness. When I experience them, I know what life is all about. The world stops and I see it; my mind goes *pow* and I see the total truth, beyond pain and pleasure, beyond right and wrong, beyond good and bad—all levels of reality without judgment, with no investment in how things turn out.

Between those moments I have my illusions to keep me warm—my dreams, hopes, fears, ego, daily routines. The world revolves around people playing on the personality level to defend their egos against other egos. The highest moments of life for me come when I transcend my ego and personality games, when I feel in my gut that the real me is—you; and that the real you is—me.

I have learned from every experience I had in the consciousness movement; each trip has taught me to enjoy what I am doing while doing it. The growth movement has become a new school system across America, an informal network of people teaching each other, the Easternizing of American aggressive energy. What's important is how well the teaching is integrated into our beings.

At thirty-seven I am now growing (up), coming to

terms with myself, accepting my limitations. I say (up) because I do not feel that I was immature or adolescent when I was active in the 1960's protesting the Vietnam War. We were childlike in our enthusiasm and idealism, and I never want to lose that sense of awe and excitement. Yet we acted like we had all the answers, and we didn't. As I grow older I am learning how much I do not know about life. I am still searching like a child for security and total happiness when it does not exist. I will still be growing (up) on my death bed. The moment I think I know all about life, I find out I know nothing. That's growing (up).

Chapter 15
Dear "Abbie"

(Abbie Hoffman was arrested in August, 1973, by New York police and charged with the sale of cocaine. If convicted, he would have been sent to jail for a mandatory fifteen years to life. Rather than stand trial, he disappeared underground, a fugitive from justice.)

Dear Abbie:

It feels so strange writing. I want to pick up the phone and hear your laughing voice at the other end, that voice that communicates total excitement.

190

Wherever you are—forced to live on the lam in your own country, to leave your wife and child to avoid almost certain life imprisonment—I know you are laughing. I feel like wallowing in self-pity, but your spirit won't let me. I see you laughing at the existential comedy of your situation, turning every negative into a positive adventure.

I love you, Abbie. You helped free me. You taught me that life can be fun. When we were doing yippie together, I feared you too much to love you. I feared you because of my own insecurity and paranoia. Because I did not feel I was as funny or as captivating, I competed with you in order to prove to you, to other people—and to myself—that I was as good. I admired you too much to love you.

Remember when we sat stoned in your living room and plotted the downfall of Lyndon Baines Johnson? We were crazy: We knew that we had the media genius to plot events that would help drive him out of office! Remember laughing together, knowing we believed enough in ourselves to take on the United States government—and win? Remember jumping up and down and exclaiming, "Isn't life fun!" We didn't go along with the movement people who thought that being politically serious meant that you couldn't have any fun.

We liked to think big, globally. We plotted world and national revolution. We wanted to remake the world and create a place of love, sharing, equality. We knew in our guts how bloody, money-hungry, and hypocritical the people who run this country are.

You are a genuine American humorist, social critic, and revolutionary. It was such an experience to grow and build with you—to watch yippie evolve from an idea to a household word. Wow! How did we all pull it off?

I will never ever forget those incredible days sitting next to you at the table at the Chicago trial. What an actor! What theater! You were so funny and your humor was so powerful because it was so dramatic, real, to the point—it forced everyone to reveal themselves.

I know, Abbie, that you didn't let many people see your deep, serious nature. Everything you did had a political purpose. You are truly a Zen master. You not only had ideas, you implemented them. You never felt yourself above running a mimeograph machine, cleaning a room, cooking a meal, writing a leaflet. You were a tireless worker as well as an inventive genius, and it was sometimes tough for me to keep up with your energy.

Abbie, those were beautiful days and crazy times. We quarreled in public and private on political and personal levels, forcing people to choose between us. We advocated socialism and cooperation and we competed in our own daily process. We didn't trust each other. We were magnetically and publicly linked. We influenced each other so much that it was sometimes hard for us to be together. We avoided appearing before the media together because our competition, jealousy, and pure energy was too powerful. It was like having a twin. People called me "Abbie" and you "Jerry."

Yes, we were media casualties! We let the media tear apart our relationship. We competed for attention like media junkies after a fix. As the movement died,

I felt my competition dying down, and my self-respect and respect for you rising. I felt great as we began to develop a close friendship independent of politics. One part of you did not want to see the movement die—you wanted to take the struggle to even deeper levels. Another part of you mellowed out, as you moved to the country, loved to cook, spent time alone with your son, america, and developed a growing beautiful relationship with Anita. It was beautiful visiting you. You were happy. Really happy. You dug playing with your boy and dog, and cooking, and gardening.

During this period, we were both attacked in print, you more than me. I tried to understand the people who attacked you. I knew they didn't know you. You are too sincere, open, and loving a person to warrant those crazy attacks. Your name became a symbol of freedom—which is threatening to people who prefer to remain unfree. The contradictions within the country, plus confusion and jealousy, led people to want to destroy your name—it was too threatening. They said, "See, *even* Abbie Hoffman is rich and bourgeois," in order to eliminate you as a potential mirror for them to see their lives. The media that built you joined with the misled, jealous, and scared people to attack you.

It was hard to find anyone who would say a good word about us then. After all, we were evil incarnate: males, strong images, and famous to boot. Movement people attacked us unmercifully in the press, but when they saw us on the streets they acted friendly, as if nothing had been written. They didn't know that we hurt too.

I saw us move out of youth-oriented yippie consciousness to think of ourselves as parents, adults, mature men. I had always feared aging, as I know you did. I associated getting older with getting sick. We meant literally all those youth-oriented statements we made as yippies. They were appropriate then. But I actually enjoy getting older. I have become happier. I feel better than I have at any time in my life.

I want to be politically active again—but not at the expense of my happiness and health. I do not want to be in a crazy movement that psychologically drains its people. I know that many ex-political people feel this way. We want to be active again, but in a new way. We want people to relate to each other in the movement in an intimate, nonmechanical way. We remember how the movement used and destroyed personal relationships.

People are important to us, as is our health and mental peace. We hate imperialism as much as before, but now we are serious about being and living the human alternative. We want our lives to be models for ourselves and others. We are not into sacrifice, martyrdom.

Remember the last time we saw each other, at the Dick Cavett Show? Since then I have been in heavy self-analysis. It's self-survival. Before therapy, I didn't know where my parents ended and I began. Remember how sensitive I used to be to criticism? These days I feel like a growing person. I no longer have to prove anything to anyone, not even to myself.

As I grow older, I get closer and closer to the little boy in me. I treat my little child with the same kind of love that I wanted as a child. Of course, I still have my hang-ups and problems. But there is a big difference. Now I allow myself to feel my hang-ups and problems, and I do not freak out. I take them as opportunities for growth.

I'll never forget that 1 A.M. phone call from New York to San Francisco telling me that you had been busted. After the call, I reread a letter you had written me a month before your frame-up. Abbie, you "saw" it all psychically! You wrote:

"Anita and I are in ecstasy out here. Our vegetable garden is beautiful; america and butterscotch are perfect—our love grows strongly in the summer sun. It's so idyllic we expect some great tragedy since Life, we fear, wasn't meant to be this great. Who knows?"

Three months later you get busted and are driven underground, away from your wife Anita, son america, dog butterscotch, vegetable garden, and summer love—how ironic life can be.

We always have to fight the self-destructive urge within ourselves. Abbie, who knows what incredible internal psychic factors have driven you underground? I believe that we get what we want out of life. Perhaps you are where you want to be.

It is hard to accept separation. As soon as I make a deep friendship I lose it. I guess the only way to keep an old friend is by making a new one. Rhoda and I were inseparable in action and consciousness for two years and now we've gone our separate ways. Ruthie and I lived together for five years—now there is no on-going contact. Stew and I have been living at opposite ends of the country. And now you and me, Abbie. When will we see each other again? Is this what is meant by growing old? People go different ways. But we will always be together, I know, because

195

our spirits are always together. And I miss your god damn physical presence too, Abbie! I love you and I miss you.

I know that what we were part of in the 1960's will return in some other form. Wouldn't it be far-out if we could build a movement based on positive self-love and love for everyone without destructive infighting? A movement that always tells the truth, that communicates love and positive vibes, that fights injustice with humanity and love. Our movement will be a model of the society we want to build, and the people we are becoming.

And you, Abbie? One wrong move and you could be behind bars the rest of your life. Oh, how that would crush us, your friends, as much as you. Lay low and enjoy your life. You'll be able to come back someday. We will see to that. Wherever you are, take care of yourself. Eat well. Get plenty of sleep. Water the plants. Stay high. You have so many people who love you. I love you.

Jerry

Chapter 16

Uniting the Personal and the Political

URING the past few years there has been a widespread feeling of powerlessness in our country, and people have put aside collective solutions in favor of individual pursuits. I have experienced the general consciousness changes within myself. Today I am more apathetic, cynical, and individualistic than I was a decade ago; nevertheless, I am still optimistic, idealistic, and believe in collective action.

Friends ask me, "Isn't your inward growth trip an escape from social reality?" Yes, it's a far cry from leading a march on the Pentagon to sitting cross-legged, counting my breaths. But there is no contradiction. We activists in the 1960's eventually lost touch with ourselves. Arica, est, bioenergetics, and other growth trips are geared to creating a centered individual who moves politically from a deep place. Dissatisfaction is not the only source for political action; people can be political from a personally satisfied place.

In the sixties I stressed one part of my being—the traditionally "masculine" part—the achieving "doer"—while underemphasizing the other part—the "feminine," accepting "be-er." My vision of the model human being was a totally committed person fighting against oppression, willing to sacrifice his life and freedom for the people.

In the consciousness movement of the seventies I have a new vision: a loving person, without expectations, who lives in his senses and in the moment.

These two ideals are not contradictory, although they represent different poles of my psyche. The political vision implies struggle; the psychic vision, harmony. In a synthesis I can create harmony through struggle, and be harmonious while struggling.

As the consciousness movement expands, its natural evolution will be toward changing society, taking the new energy generated through meditation, yoga, honesty, and self-awareness outward into social institutions.

We can take our self-awareness techniques and make them available to the American people through street theater, free schools; programs in factories, ghettoes, jails, and churches; political activism; the mass media; even demonstrations.

We are headed for another "do it" period. Perhaps the 1980's will see the activism of the sixties combined with the awareness of the seventies. In the next flurry of activity we will come from a deeper psychological and spiritual base.

The psychological-spiritual experimentation is a natural evolution from the activist political explosion. Standing on the edge of history between past and future, we are pioneers without road maps. We have an opportunity to transform the planet, but first we need to free ourselves from the conditioning of the past and find our natural internal harmony; to lower our defenses and establish our common humanity.

The rebellion of the sixties was a declaration of independence by a young generation against its elders. It was so pervasive that even those whom the rebellion did not directly touch were apologetic about their distance from the rebellion while its symbols and language have been adopted by the society at large. The rebellion itself represented a dramatic break from social programming. We received one programming, recognized its irrelevance, and consciously began to design another.

We are not yet the people we want to be. The people now in their twenties and thirties, the generation that attacked the government in the streets in the 1960's, are a transitional generation. We are redefining what it means to be post-thirty, and soon will redefine what being forty, fifty, and "old" means. We are redefining the values of society, from marriage to family to work to love and death.

Nothing is taken for granted anymore. All the old definitions and social forms are losing their energy. The hippie revolt foreshadowed this awakening. Many

199

hippies have since dropped back into society and now it is their parents who are dropping out. "Solid citizens" are asking themselves, "Even if I 'make it,' so what?"

America is experiencing a spiritual rebirth as people discover that a materialistic existence, an ego-dominated life, is unsatisfying. We are looking for meaning in our life, pleasure in our bodies, and honest communication rather than image, money, or power. This decline in chasing after symbols and objects is eroding the morale of capitalism.

The consciousness revolution is climaxing with the liberation of women and the feminization of men. All definitions of what "men" and "women" do are up for grabs today, as questions of biology vs. social conditioning are being worked out in homes, offices, and schools.

The consciousness movement is bringing Eastern philosophies to the West, modifying the aggressive, masculine, control philosophies of Western industrialism. Our traditional, competitive outlook effectively industrialized the West, but it does not work in the atomic age where sharing and distribution are bigger problems than production. For this era a new value system is needed. We are importing Zen, yoga, and Buddhism and combining them with our emphasis on technology, achievement, and control over nature, in a new synthesis of East and West.

The growth movement must also grow. It must eliminate its internal contradictions of authoritarianism, sexism, economic barriers, spiritual escapism. The men got kicked out by women as political leaders in the 1960's, so they came back as gods. The movement is heavily dominated by male gurus who use spiritual evolution to justify authoritarianism. Spiritual groups see people on different steps of a consciousness ladder; therefore, disciples choose to follow the word of swamis and yogis higher on the ladder . . . even to the kissing of rings and feet.

Financially, the high cost of therapy effectively keeps it a white middle-class activity out of the reach of the economically oppressed. Thus, the consciousness movement does not make itself available to the powerless. It has become another service for white middle-class society.

Is it self-indulgent to work on your own psychological pain while starvation and physical terror punish millions of people in the world? Although it does not intrinsically follow that an inward search must lead to political indifference, at this stage in the consciousness movement people are overreacting to what they perceive as the failure of the movement in the 1960's.

At the moment, therefore, the consciousness movement is not addressing itself to problems of economic inequality, political torture, war and peace. Until it does, it will be incomplete. No spiritual movement can claim to deal with the suffering of humanity if it neglects physical oppression.

The growth movement talks a lot about loving yourself and loving God, but it says very little about loving specific human beings that you have never met and have no direct relationship with, e.g., black people in jail, South African miners, Indian peasants, Bolivian Indians, and Vietnamese.

Going inward to find yourself or experience "the truth" is no alternative to political action. The economic necessities of life determine consciousness more decisively than any spiritual program. A high political consciousness is as important as a high psychological or spiritual consciousness. Spirituality without struggle, high consciousness without compassion, leads nowhere.

The answer is not for oppressed peoples to solve their problems through therapy, spirituality, or health foods, but to analyze their own condition and organize for their rights and power. Whatever the consciousness movement does to aid that process is important. The consciousness movement must serve the people, and not be just another diversion from alienation.

The know-yourself movement can be a self-indulgent, escapist, individualistic alternative to collective activity. The individual, at odds with nature and society, tries to become one with himself as a final salvation. But I don't believe anyone can attain self-perfection in a vacuum. I am no higher than the society around me. I have a responsibility to oppressed people as well as to myself.

We know from history that the powerful give up their power only when forced to. The rise in consciousness and the organization of working and poor people is what is going to equalize America, not changes from the top. The consciousness movement will work to the extent that it reaches millions and millions of Americans through the mass media and through political alternatives.

In the sixties we exposed the degree to which external institutions controlled us and created poverty, injustice, and alienation. The seventies have been a somersault: "I am responsible for my own condition." This self-responsibility has liberated people to work from within to change social institutions. We are all victims. But as long as we see ourselves as victims, we stay victims. Only when we take total responsibility for our own situation can we begin to free ourselves. We are responsible for our individual karma and awareness, and at the same time, we are each responsible for the condition of the planet, including hunger, suffering, poverty, oppression.

Political activists often say that spirituality diminishes activism, cools out rebellion, and diverts people from the day-by-day struggle. But that is not an inevitable function of spirituality. A healthy philosophy about our earth should include its relationship to the universe. A belief in reincarnation should not conflict with a desire to create a just society on earth. Keeping meditation nonpolitical is an unconscious acceptance of the feudal roots of the philosophy in peasant societies. Spiritual religions must grow with the times.

The New Consciousness movement has the potential to unite spirituality and politics. There are many spiritually minded people who dismiss the physical world as illusion, just as there are many political people who deny the spiritual. More and more people today, however, are interested both in spiritual evolution *and* positive social change.

Using a spiritual approach in political ways may change people in ways we never before imagined. The future belongs to the people who have the largest view of the potential of human beings, not to those with the narrowest. A revolutionary must have the most positive view of human nature. Out of that view he acts, creates, and influences behavior.

Jerry Rubin

I have a positive vision that America will peacefully elect a politically humanistic government. The media, the electrical hot-spring of the nation, creates awareness revolutions every second. The institutions of democracy—voting, free discussion of issues, media reporting—work for the people. America moves to the left. The fall of the empire is matched by a spiritual rebirth. The spirit of freedom when loose in the land cannot be contained.

What happens after a peaceful positive change is another matter. In 1971, I spent two months in Chile with Stew Albert and Phil Ochs, observing the first Latin American country to elect a Marxist president and implement socialist economic change through constitutional means. We debated the future of this unique social experiment. Stew felt the CIA would never allow the Chilean experiment to succeed. He also felt that it was impossible to make large-scale economic changes non-violently. I thought Chile's tradition of democracy would eliminate the possibility of a military coup and hoped that the rich might voluntarily give up their privileges to help the poor.

Two years later, the middle class deserted Allende. The military invaded the government house and assassinated him. They bombed radical factories and the university, jailed thousands, and imposed a repressive junta. The CIA sabotaged the socialist economy by financing crippling strikes and feeding money to the junta. I went to Chile to learn about the democratic implementation of socialism; instead, I learned about violence, selfishness, and America's role in the world.

The time has come for people to leave their roles and "points-of-view" for a new vision of the human being and society. It is time to politically apply the values of high consciousness—health, honesty, awareness, responsibility, aliveness, sharing, and love.

The millions of people who are involved in deliberate alterations of consciousness will have political effects in the mellowing of America. A political movement will emerge out of the awareness revolution to implement the new consciousness.

The world is a village; our fates are intertwined. What happens in a rural town in India affects a suburb in Indiana. The individualistic, competitive philosophies of the past no longer work in the present era of international technology, communication, and travel. At the moment many people have pessimistically given up the idea of creating a "healthy society." Cynicism runs deep. We feel sold out by left and right. The New Consciousness movement can rescue people from this cynicism; it can transform suspicion into optimism. People are scared to open themselves up again for fear of being hurt, but the positive feelings are there; what is needed is a movement to bring them out.

The world is moving toward the sharing of wealth and power, and the emergence of oppressed minorities to power. If America joins that trend instead of resisting it, we will discover a new motivation for our lives. We now feel that we have lost our way, that history is passing us by. But this process can be reversed by going in the same direction as history. We have the technology and soul to give much to the world if we can overcome our obsession with our power, and transcend our fear. Fear holds America back and perpetuates the very things that we are afraid of.

Jerry Rubin

America needs intensive internal therapy to read-just its views and power relationships. America must go inward to rediscover itself, not to become self-absorbed and isolationist, but to share and give in a healthy way with the world. To do that the American people will have to share more equally because we will have less. That requires a power change within the United States away from the large corporations and to the mass of the people.

The new movement will base itself on the equality of all human beings, putting into active practice the things learned about the body, mind, and spirit. A new health philosophy will expand the minds of doctors. A new body awareness will teach people to take responsibility for their own health. A political movement, directly related to people's basic needs from food to health to creative work, will emerge.

The New Consciousness movement will address itself to humanizing jails and ghettoes, abolishing poverty, serving the needs of old and sick people, creating a healthy social environment, controlling pollution, turning the nation into one big encounter and growth group.

The movement sees its role as service: everyone takes responsibility for everyone else. We accept that we have an effect on each other. We serve each other and all gain. The goal of life will be experience, rather than material possessions. The movement will be an alternative family as well as political organization.

Today, I am interested in relations between people, in personal growth, in spiritual questions—as well as political and economic questions. I see the need for collective action, confrontation, and transfer of power from the few to the many. I don't think that any changes in society can be implemented without collective political change. Unless the economic level of society is made democratic, people have a practical and a psychological motivation to be selfish. But one changes the political-economic level by concentrating also on the personal, spiritual, and consciousness level of life.

In the 1960's we postponed all questions on personal growth until after the revolution. But revolution is only as high as the people that make it. I had expected the revolution apocalyptically, but have since discovered that revolution is an evolutionary process. I am also a process. My personal growth and your personal growth match the growth of mass consciousness. People out of touch with bodies and souls cannot make positive change. Political activism without self-awareness perpetuates cycles of anger, competition, ego battles.

The potential of spiritual discipline is the ability to break people from programming and attachments. People think they are their paychecks, homes, jobs, power positions, children. The spiritual movement has the potential of getting people in touch with the essence beyond the things they identify with. Then people may take actions which free themselves from the things that run their lives. The spiritual movement can be revolutionary not by preaching, but by giving people a new experience.

The human body is resistant, but change is possible, people do grow. The spiritual is catching up with the technological. We are reaching a new potential within ourselves for control over our bodies, our awareness, and our health. On a profound level the world is going through a massive evolution of consciousness.

Using myself as a guinea pig, I am trying to learn

to give up my negative games, my defenses, the mechanisms I use to survive. Before I can change other people, I must change myself. I am now working on myself to become a spiritually high, nonattached human being. When I do that, I will be able to share with other people, and will become a true spiritual psychological revolutionary.

The consciousness movement and the political movement have a lot to learn from one another. A fusion of the two will create the healthy balance, politicizing the growth movement and providing a spiritual and psychological base for politics. An organic relationship exists. Many people are merging all levels of their beings, political, emotional, sexual, economic, psychological. For the first time in history we are talking about creating the total human being on a mass scale, as we develop ourselves in all aspects of our being.